I WILL SEE YOU
IN FAR OFF PLACES

Áine Ní Cheallaigh

PHOTO CREDITS

Massive thanks to all the fans who contributed their photographs for use in this book:

Alyssa pgs 34, 52, 54, 65, 69, 110, 132, 137, 141, 163, 181, 190, 232
Karina Ruiz Angelo pgs 126, 210, 211, 212, 214
Daniela Leiva pgs 148, 158, 160, 164, 166
Grace Bizzell pgs 17, 20 (#1), 30, 31
Ricardo Martinez pgs 26, 32, 36, 41
Vanessa Kíntopp pgs 230, 231 (#2), 234, 235
Renata Spinola pgs 107, 112, 115
Diego G. Siegels pgs 202, 207, 209
Elina Roddick pg 15 (#1, #2)
Camila Toloza G. pg 66
Annylin Cea pg 88
Trinity White pg 91
Gustavo from Paraguay pg 161
Luz Ángela Almonte pg 177 (#1)
Victoria Schwindt pg 180

Additional material came from:

Movistar TV pgs 61, 62, 68, 70, 85 (#2), 89, 90
Beto Landoni pgs 176, 177 (#2)
Ariel Fuentes Muñoz pg 58
Unknown photographer pg 86
Teatro Renault pg 93
Sean McGonagle pg 123 (#2)
Slug Solos/Tumblr pg 192 (#1)

And endless thanks to Nora for taking about 40 of the remaining pictures in this book. I couldn't have done this without you ♥

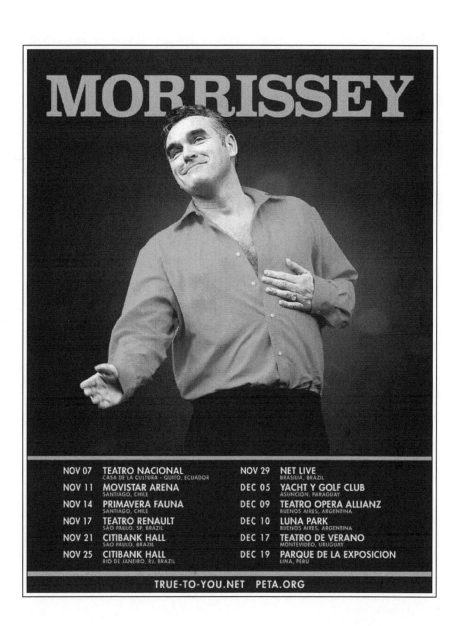

MORRISSEY

NOV 07	**TEATRO NACIONAL** CASA DE LA CULTURA - QUITO, ECUADOR	NOV 29	**NET LIVE** BRASILIA, BRAZIL
NOV 11	**MOVISTAR ARENA** SANTIAGO, CHILE	DEC 05	**YACHT Y GOLF CLUB** ASUNCION, PARAGUAY
NOV 14	**PRIMAVERA FAUNA** SANTIAGO, CHILE	DEC 09	**TEATRO OPERA ALLIANZ** BUENOS AIRES, ARGENTINA
NOV 17	**TEATRO RENAULT** SÃO PAULO, SP, BRAZIL	DEC 10	**LUNA PARK** BUENOS AIRES, ARGENTINA
NOV 21	**CITIBANK HALL** SAO PAULO, BRAZIL	DEC 17	**TEATRO DE VERANO** MONTEVIDEO, URUGUAY
NOV 25	**CITIBANK HALL** RIO DE JANEIRO, RJ, BRAZIL	DEC 19	**PARQUE DE LA EXPOSICION** LIMA, PERU

TRUE-TO-YOU.NET   PETA.ORG

INTRODUCTION

I don't speak Spanish. Sure, I've picked up a dozen words or so, how could I avoid it, living in New York City for 10 years. Hola is hello. Uno, dos, tres, cuatro. Hasta mañana, see you tomorrow.

In September of 2015, I picked up a whole other set of words: website Spanish. My wife and I were going to South America, following all of Morrissey's tour, and if we were going to see the whole tour, we would need tickets for all twelve shows. Buscar, search. Próximamente, coming soon. Comprar, buy. Retiro en punto de venta, pick up at the ticket office.

My wife Nora and I were both writers, quiet introverts, stay-at-home bookish types. (She's the one on the left). 'Adventurous' was not a word that leapt to mind when describing either of us. But in our late 30s, things had changed. I had embarked on a journey of self-discovery, a spiritual path that had shown me that my true self was less of a bookworm and more of a rocker than I had ever imagined. Nora's path had been a harder one. Her mother had recently died of cancer. It had made Nora reassess her life, think about what kinds of

things were really important, what kinds of things people might regret on their deathbeds.

We were both devoted Morrissey fans—Nora for the comfort his music had given her during her mother's long illness and in her time of grief, and me for the inspiration he'd provided for my creative journey. There was no way that we would turn around at the end of our lives and say that we'd seen him too often. And so we decided to spend Nora's inheritance from her mother on following Morrissey, taking the leap, embarking on the grand adventure of seeing a whole tour, while also seeing South America for the first time in our lives.

Now it was October, and things were getting serious. We needed to make a plan, an itinerary. The twelve shows were spread out over six weeks in seven countries. The distances between some of them were mammoth. Trains were not a thing in South America. If you were broke, you took a long-haul bus from place to place, often overnight, or even over a period of days, but in our case, we were going to fly.

It was no joke to book 13 flights and 14 hotels. Once they were booked, there was no going back, so we really needed to answer crucial questions like, Do we want to spend the days between the Santiago and São Paulo shows in Chile or Brazil? What to base the decision on? All I knew about Chile was I'd met a kid from there once when I was a babysitter who said Chileans really liked hot dogs. And Brazil? Well, that was the country where they spoke Portuguese instead of Spanish. Hot dogs vs Portuguese was no kind of decision-making criterion, so some high-intensity research was in order.

It was a bit terrifying.

I am not a big risk-taker. In personality terms, I am self-preservation dominant, which means that I instinctively keep my physical health and safety as a top priority. The more I researched, the less safe I felt. Quito, Ecuador, our first stop, was okay, as long as you never took busses. There were children who were trained to wriggle under bus seats and steal your bag when you weren't looking. Oh, and as long as you didn't walk around at night in the historical district; tourists being mugged at knife-point was a common occurrence. Oh, and also as long as you didn't walk around in broad daylight. One review I read on Trip-Advisor said, My father and I loved Quito, there was the unfortunate incident where we were mugged at machete-point in the park at 3pm, but otherwise we had a great time. And then there were the stories of tourists who were kidnapped and kept for days, brought to the ATM once a day to withdraw the maximum amount from their checking account, and only released when the funds were drained.

But these were isolated incidents. Our chances of making it out of Quito unmugged and unkidnapped were quite high. But there seemed to be no chance of getting out of there without contracting a roaring case of explosive diarrhea. The water wasn't safe to drink; it wasn't even safe to brush your teeth with. I compiled a list of rules that would maybe keep us from getting sick. No street food. No salads. No ice in drinks. No juice. No strawberries. No opening your mouth while you shower.

And that was just Quito. The list of dangers in each city was different. The taxi drivers passing you bad bills in your change was what you had to watch out for in Argentina. Forgery was big business in Buenos Aires. Mosquitos biting you and giving you yellow fever was what could get you in Brasilia. I researched, I Googled, I looked each city up on TripAdvisor, I took notes.

And kept trying to learn some Spanish. At first, since I was a music lover, I figured I would learn Spanish by learning the lyrics of the most popular songs currently in the charts in the countries I was visiting in South America, but quite quickly, I saw that vocabulary phrases like, "move your hips," or "I need your kisses," weren't going to be very useful. If only there were dance tunes about determining which items on a menu were vegan, or about negotiating a taxi fare to the airport. That would have been helpful, but no.

So instead, I downloaded an app onto my iPad that taught me phrases like, Yo como arroz, I eat rice, Mi camisa es amarillo, my shirt is yellow, and what turned out to be the most useful phrase of all, El mono bebe jugo, the monkey drinks juice.

El mono.

There were twelve shows spread out over a period of six weeks, but the shows were not evenly spaced. There were a couple of gaps where we had four or five days to entertain ourselves, take side trips.

And I had read a review on TripAdvisor, a description of a hotel. It was placed in the middle of the jungle, within walking distance of one of the most spectacular waterfalls in the world. In this hotel, the most important thing that staff reminded you to do was to close the sliding door of your balcony, because if you didn't, the monkeys living in the surrounding jungle would come into your room, open the minibar, and steal your juice.

El mono bebe jugo!

Oh how my heart longed to stay in this magical hotel! Monkeys were so fun, I loved them. But zoos were so depressing, I hated them and never went anymore. Could it really be possible to go to a place where monkeys lived in the wild? To see them in their home, their natural habitat. If you stayed at the Sheraton Iguazu, it apparently was.

I presented my case for the Sheraton Iguazu side trip to Nora and she agreed. Hooray! She presented her case for a side trip to Salvador in Brazil and I agreed. Salvador was a place Nora had learned about in college when she'd taken a Brazilian Studies class. I didn't even need to hear what it was like. It was a place Nora had wanted to visit for 20 years, and so we were going. Because Nora had taken this class on Brazil, she had some concept of what it was like, and so when it came to research, I dubbed her The Boss of All Brazil, and left her to look up everything besides the basics of 1) would brushing our teeth with the water make us violently ill? (no) 2) would taxi drivers cheat/rob us (no) and 3) were there any monkeys living in the wild that we could visit (yes! In Rio! On a path leading to a hill called Sugarloaf.)

One last side trip needed to be hammered down, and then the outlines of our trip were set. This was to Machu Picchu in Peru. This was something my heart longed to see even more than monkeys. I had been to Egypt, seen the pyramids, the Great Sphinx, the temples, the statues, and had fallen deeply in love with the art and architecture of those people who had lived thousands and thousands of years ago. If Morrissey had thrown his arms around Paris, I had with equal fervor thrown my arms around ancient Egypt, and I had recently read a book that posited that the creators of the Egyptian pyramids were the same stone-working superbeings who had predated the Incans, creating the extremely Egyptian-looking foundations of Machu Picchu.

Peru was the last stop on our trip, and Nora really, really wanted to be home before her late grandmother's birthday on December 23rd so she could spend it with her family. I wheedled an extra two days out of her, and booked complex trains and hard-to-buy non-refundable Machu Picchu tickets for December 20th and 21st, days so far in advance, it seemed impossible that we would ever arrive at them with this itinerary still intact.

Blam, blam, blam, each city, the hotel, the flight, printing it out, adding it to the travel folder. It all went fine, except for an awful moment when I went to book our room at the Yacht y Golf Club in Paraguay and it looked like the hotel was sold out. As soon as this venue was announced, inexplicably, I had taken it into my heart and had even more tender longing feelings towards it than I did for el mono. The city of Asunción in Paraguay was really the runt of the tour. It was the only landlocked country we were visiting, and Asunción, God bless it, wasn't any kind of tourist destination. But the Yacht y Golf Club, if the website was anything to go by, was the fanciest place in town. It was trying so hard, it was so endearing. It made no sense, I can't explain it, my heart just knew that something special was going to happen there. I tried to picture what it could be, and came up with the awesomeness of the venue being part of the hotel. All of us Americans on the tour would naturally be staying there, and probably Morrissey and the band and the crew too. Maybe we would all hang out at the bar, the whole weekend would be a Morrissey party, what fun.

I managed to find a room at the Yacht y Golf Club and texted

Alyssa to let her know that they were going fast. She was a hardcore superfan who had been following Morrissey a couple of years longer than we had and was far more connected to the community of fans than we were. She was an extremely glamorous, super competent young woman, and even though she was just 24 years old, it made me feel much better about the trip knowing that she'd be there. If anything goes wrong, I told myself in the dark moments of worry in the middle of the night, if anyone gives us any kind of trouble, we'll set Alyssa on them and she'll do some serious buttkicking and sort everything out.

I told her I was glad she was doing the whole tour along with us, and she texted back and said that there was just a total of five of us Americans doing the whole thing: me, her, Nora, and two young longtime fans Trinity and Chayane.

I was very taken aback by this news. In my fantasies of the party at the bar of the Yacht y Golf Club, I pictured at least a dozen of us regular fans, plus the usual handful of VIPs from Morrissey's guest list. But Alyssa explained that a lot of people were put off by the fact that Morrissey's last attempt to tour South America in 2013 had been aborted. He had arrived in Lima and (what? Perhaps opened his mouth while he showered?) Before the first show, he had developed an illness so severe (I gleaned from a garbled Google-translated South American interview) they had threatened to treat him with a blood transfusion

Alyssa, Trinity and Chayane had all been there in 2013. They had all arrived in Lima full of hope, they had all taken in the disappointing news that the Lima gig was canceled. Then they had all taken the dreadful blow, the whole tour was canceled, it was time to go home. All their high hopes, thousands of dollars, down the drain.

But that wasn't stopping them from coming back for this tour. And me? I hadn't even been a Morrissey fan in 2013. Nora and I were fresh newbies, hearts full of hope. All we could do was trust that everything would turn out all right. That a miracle would happen, that nobody would get sick, that we all of us, Nora, Morrissey and I would all turn up at all twelve gigs. That we'd make it out of Quito unrobbed, we'd get to Brazil to see el mono, the party at the Yacht y Golf Club would become a reality, and the whole tour, all of us, would make it triumphant and safe to the last show, Lima, where everything would be redeemed.

It was a beautiful dream.

And so here we go. This is what actually happened in reality…

NOVEMBER 7, 2015
TEATRO NACIONAL CCE
QUITO, ECUADOR

I fell in love with Quito as soon as our plane taxied up to the jet bridge at Mariscal Sucre International Airport. Looking out the window, all down the line, jet bridge after jet bridge was emblazoned with a word that that I'd never heard before I'd started buying tickets for this tour, and associated 100% with Morrissey: Movistar. The show next week in Santiago, Chile was going to be held at a venue called Movistar Arena. The second Santiago show was at a festival called Movistar Primavera Fauna.

I turned on my phone, and in the corner, the name of the local network I was connecting to appeared: Movistar. Not just an arena then, it was a South American cellphone carrier.

I walked through the Movistar jet bridge and grinned at the big green M as I passed it. This was it, the end of the planning phase and the beginning of those plans actually becoming real. My heart sang.

The ride from the airport, punctuated by Movistar billboards, was peaceful and serene. Quito unfolded itself outside the windows of the cab for us to see. Tall mountains, covered with a

carpet of deep green. Houses, they looked like no more than colorful little boxes, stacked up the side of each mountain, as far as
one could feasibly go. We drove on into the valley, into the heart
of Quito and arrived in the narrow cobbled streets of the historical district where our hotel was. I had prepared fake wallets for
us to carry around and hand to muggers if the occasion arose
and we had them ready in our pockets as we walked out to dinner that night, but it didn't feel necessary. Quito felt safe, the very
stones of the streets seemed to welcome us.

"Remember, no ice, no salads,
no tap water," I said to Nora as we
walked into the restaurant.

"Yeah, yeah," she said, and we sat
and puzzled over the menu, typing
things into the Google translate app
on my phone to try to figure it all out.

We ordered our food, and I gave
Nora an absolutely mystified look
when she ordered a juice! With
strawberries in it!

"What are you doing?" I said.
"No juice!"

"Oh I forgot," she said. "Well, I won't drink it." That was when we first realized that Quito's altitude was having an effect. We neither of us had any unpleasant headache or weakness, but that night, we both felt notably woolly-minded. It was a relief to know that that was going to be the extent of it.

Our hotel was a lovely historical building where a glass roof had been placed over the central courtyard that now housed the restaurant. There was live traditional music over dinner and the sound of it carried up to our room. Pan pipes and guitar were not top of my list when it came to musical ensembles, but there was something appropriate about hearing this music in the land that it actually came from, not on a New York City subway platform. As I drifted off to sleep, I realized that I recognized the song I was hearing; it was Simon and Garfunkel's El Condor Pasa. Wait, did this mean that Paul  Simon hadn't written the music for that song? Had he just cribbed a traditional melody? Were the hammer and the nail and the sparrow and the snail just a rip-off of the original Spanish lyrics too? I fell asleep and forgot all about looking it up.

In the morning, the first order of business was to pick up our Morrissey tickets. I had naturally ordered the tickets for all 12 of the shows online, but only four of the shows, the Brazilian ones, had offered a print-at-home ticket option. A few of the others had a pretty normal pick-up-at-the-box office option, but the rest were really odd. Apparently in a lot of South American countries, it was standard to pick up your ticket for a show, not at the venue, but at various locations that were often in far-flung places

quite far from the venue. Often they were supermarkets; in Buenos Aires, it was an OCA (I still wasn't quite sure what an OCA
was, maybe something like a FedEx office?) and sometimes they
just seemed to be random locations sandwiched between two
landmarks (perhaps a little ticket booth on the side of the road?)
It was all very hard to parse from my office at home in New York
using the very limited powers of Google translate.

I brought my passport, in my money belt naturally, to fox the
thieves. It was apparently hard to buy anything more than a stick
of gum in South America without presenting your passport as
proof of identity. And we set off in a taxi that our hotel had called
for us (no hailing taxis in Quito off the street!) and made our way
to a store called Almacenes Rickie. I had chosen this location because I had seen on Google maps that there was a Swissotel next
door. The taxi we'd catch back from there quite likely wouldn't
try to rip us off or kidnap us.

"So what kind of store is this?" Nora asked me in the taxi.

"Maybe like a Home Depot?" I said. "Kind of a hardware
store? That also sells jewelry? And concert tickets?"

"Yeah?"

"I really don't know,"
I said, giving up. "We'll
just have to see."

And when we walked
in the door, we saw
exactly what kind of
store Almacenes Rickie
was. It was the store of
dreams. It wasn't hugely
big, it felt like a small-
town department store
from my childhood in
Ireland, but it didn't at all

have a crowded feel. Each item of stock was laid out attractively. Each item was something really worth wanting: an electric guitar, a grand piano, the most elaborate grandfather clock I had ever seen, a silver statue of a zebra the size of a poodle. As we walked to the back of the store where the ticket counter was, we passed the expensive watches, the display cases of jewelry, the diesel generators, the refrigerators. And after waiting on line, we presented the printout of my confirmation email and my passport to the woman behind the window who didn't speak a word of English, and waited for her to make our dream come true.

Before I had left on this trip, I had talked to my friend Sarah about the time she had spent in Ecuador working on a farm. After describing the roaring case of explosive diarrhea she'd contracted, she'd talked about how incredibly kind the people of Ecuador were.

"They will always help you," she said. "Everywhere we went, in stores, strangers on the street, they would always stop and help us, no matter what."

I'd found that description really hard to reconcile with the mental picture I was carrying around of Ecuadorians as hardened crooks who trained their children to rob you on busses. I chalked it up to the fact that Sarah was one of the most softhearted people I knew, who would probably willingly hand her bag over to an Ecuadorian child-thief, figuring they needed her stuff more than she did.

But standing at that counter, watching how the woman was utterly flummoxed by our request, I began to see this Ecuadorian helpfulness first-hand. It was clear within a couple of minutes that printing out tickets ordered from the US was a request that overwhelmed the capacities of Alamcenes Rickie's alarmingly ancient computer system. But the woman behind the counter didn't waver for a second. She called over her colleague who also didn't speak English. He brought us out to a hut in the parking lot and had an exchange with a man sitting at a computer there, the upshot of which led him back inside to restart the computer a couple of times, a process that took about ten minutes each time.

Every now and then, I would look at Nora and begin to suggest that we give up and go to another of the mysterious locations in Quito where we could attempt to pick up the tickets. But she looked so calm and patient. The man and the woman, they were both clearly so utterly committed to the process of making our dream come true. I couldn't interrupt them; I just stood quietly and waited. And about 30 minutes after we had entered Almacenes Rickie, the man appeared from some mystery location with our Morrissey tickets in his hand and without any fuss handed them over to me.

"Gracias," I said, over and over. "Gracias."

We left the store and sat in the lobby of the Swissotel for a few minutes to collect ourselves. A trembling relief had swept over me and I needed to sit. It was all so tenuous. The fat folders of plane tickets and email receipts and directions to ticket pickup locations, what if I'd gotten it wrong? What if I'd misunderstood everything? What if it actually wasn't possible to pick up tickets in South America purchased online in the US? I knew I'd just done it, but the process had revealed a fear I was carrying in me. A fear that this tour wasn't really meant for the likes of us. A fear that it was just for South Americans, plus three of the hardest-core US fans, seasoned travelers who could take on anything.

But taking deep breaths in the lobby of the Swissotel, I told myself that it was happening. I was holding the tickets in my hand, Morrissey, Teatro Nacional B42 and B43. We would at least get to see him this once, here in Quito.

My ears pricked up as I heard the strains of a song I recognized, and it wasn't El Condor Pasa. A group of young men were standing at a table nearby in the lobby and one of them was playing a song on his phone. It was Suedehead. What kind of awesomeness was this? Were people standing in hotel lobbies all over Quito, hanging out, listening to Morrissey?

As we left, we purposely walked right past the group of guys, and only one of them noticed the MOZ shaved into the side of Nora's bright orange hair. He elbowed and elbowed the guy beside him, but he wasn't quick enough to catch on.

Nora and I grinned at each other as we walked out the door. Tomorrow night was going to be fun.

• • •

Doors were at 6pm, and though the show wouldn't start for ages after that, I was feeling antsy and wanted to get going. We walked the few blocks from our hotel to the Teatro Nacional Sucre, the fanciest venue in town where the symphony orchestra played, and walked into the lobby and presented our tickets.

But there was something terribly wrong. Where was everybody? The place was deserted!

The ticket-taker looked dubiously at our tickets and shook her head. She didn't speak English. She led us over to another woman who looked at our tickets and also shook her head. She didn't speak English, but she pointed us across the pretty cobblestoned square to a pair of armed security guards standing in the corner. We went over and handed them our tickets and they squinted at them and shook their heads. They didn't speak English. One of them took the tickets and disappeared into an office. While he was gone, a woman with her husband and two children came and asked a question that seemed to be about the ballet. She was still standing there when the guard came back, and she translated what he said.

"That show is not happening here," she said. "It is at another location, the Casa de la Cultura."

She took in our stricken faces.

"Don't worry," she said. "It is not far from here. A short taxi ride. Just a few dollars."

She looked at my phone and helped me locate the real venue on Google maps. Apparently there were two venues in Quito, both named the Teatro Nacional. The one we were standing in front of was the Teatro Nacional Sucre, the other was the Teatro Nacional CCE.

We thanked the woman profusely, got in a taxi and arrived at the venue still with hours to spare, but I was rattled. How many other blunders like this had I made? How could I possibly know? I hadn't officially met Chayane yet, but his parents were Mexican so he spoke fluent Spanish. I felt like asking him to sit down and leaf through our fat folders of tickets and printouts and try to spot any obvious mistakes, and maybe explain to me why the OCA in Buenos Aires needed me to pick up my tickets two business days before the event.

We got in line with all the other Morrissey fans, handed over our tickets and made our way into the theater. It was a seated show in a pretty big contemporary theater. There was a barrier between the first row of seats and the stage, and Alyssa, Trinity and Chayane were standing at the barrier. We had barely gotten to say hi to them and to Grace, another US fan who had just flown in to Quito for this one show, when security came along and shooed us all back to our seats.

Nora and I sat for a while, contemplating the familiar image projected on the screen, listening to the songs piped over the

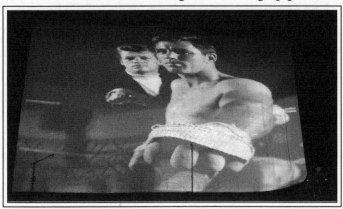

loudspeakers. These were the same songs we'd heard while waiting for so many Morrissey shows to start. In the few short years
since Nora and I had become fans, we'd managed to take in a
couple of dozen shows, most of them during Morrissey's exten-
sive tour of the US over the summer.

And here we were, so far from home, and yet on familiar
ground, back in Morrisseyland. I felt excited, nervous even, as
I thought about the upcoming show. What would happen? Having been to so many shows already, there were certain things
that were quite predictable. In about twenty minutes, the screen
would come alive and we would be treated to a montage of music videos from the past, interspersed with poetry and stand-up
comedy. At some point, either when the videos began or ended,
there would be a rush for the front, fans squeezing to fill up the
space between the barrier and the first row of seats. Front row
was the best place to be because Morrissey liked to interact with
fans, shaking hands, having little chats, or accepting notes and
flowers over the barrier.

The broad outlines of the show wouldn't be a surprise. Morrissey would quite likely begin with the song Suedehead. This
would be followed by a show that would include a lot of songs
from the latest album, World Peace Is None of Your Business.
Then the show would end, most probably, with the Smiths song,
The Queen Is Dead.

But even though the show was quite predictable in ways, there
was nothing—not a single second of any Morrissey show—that
was ho-hum or boring.

Why?

What was so amazing about Morrissey? What made him so
special?

First of all, there were the songs. Morrissey, like many songwriters, had something he was trying to convey, a message he
was trying to get across. His message was about the condition

of being human—what it was like to live, to love, to lose, to have a heart. But unlike most songwriters, Morrissey wasn't just trying. He wasn't writing hits and misses, succeeding two or three times out of ten. Morrissey had the gift of capturing something deeply resonant and true about the human heart pretty much every single time he wrote some lyrics. The language of the heart is poetry, and Morrissey had the ability to write lyrics that were the best kinds of poems, ones that were accessible enough to catch your attention half-heard over the radio at a coffee shop, and yet substantial enough that they kept supplying layer after layer of meaning hundreds of listens later.

Morrissey had been doing this for decades now. He'd started as a young man in his twenties, writing songs with his bandmate in the Smiths, guitarist Johnny Marr. Morrissey had shot to stardom in the 80s with the Smiths, and after they'd broken up after just five years together, he'd continued an equally stellar solo career, writing songs with longstanding bandmate, guitarist Boz Boorer, as well as with other bandmates who had come and gone over the years. Fans expressed personal preferences one way or the other, but it couldn't be doubted that his work with the Smiths was brilliant, and that his solo work was equally brilliant. His songs were deep, rich with meaning, a string of gems that stretched back over a long and lustrous career.

And that was just Morrissey the lyricist. Having a message to convey wasn't all there was to it. There was also the task of actually physically conveying that message. And Morrissey was utterly masterful at taking these messages of the heart and singing them not like they were something that meant something five or ten or twenty years ago, losing all meaning through repetition. He sang his songs like they were revelations arising right now from the deepest core of him that he had no choice but to express. Seeing Morrissey was not about hearing someone who was good at singing, though he did do that phenomenally well. It was about being in the presence of someone so exquisitely tuned into the reality of the heart, it opened an answering space of the heart in his listeners, giving us permission to be who we were, feel what we felt, connect to what was real.

And so the waiting ended and the action began. There was the predicted dive for the barrier. I ended up in the front row on the left, right in front of the spot where guitarist Boz Boorer would stand. Nora was standing directly behind me.

On the screen, the videos had begun. My favorite one was of French singer Charles Aznavour singing Emmenez-Moi. The song was about the longing of the heart to be elsewhere, but you didn't have to understand a word of French to understand that. His liquid brown eyes, his aching voice, his every gesture spoke it loud and clear.

If Charles Aznavour was on the screen, Morrissey was just a few short videos away. I calmed and centered myself by doing a simple meditation practice, focusing on my heart and sending thoughts of loving kindness towards the people around me, towards fans and security guards, and sending it backstage too, to the band, and to Morrissey. This was something that Nora and I did before each show. It was part of our routine, and it really helped prepare the heart for the intense emotional experience that Morrissey shows often turned out to be.

And so the videos came to an end, dramatic operatic music began to play, the stage was revealed, and out came Morrissey and the band. The audience gave him a super-effusive welcome—people were cheering, jumping up and down, waving, screaming in delight. They were echoing everything I was feeling. It was always, always, always so amazing to see him, my heart just bursting with delight.

"Hola, Quito!" Morrissey said, taking the microphone, and then we were off with Suedehead.

"Why do you come here?" Morrissey sang.

More cheers, more delighted screams in response. So many people around us were singing along.

"And why?" he continued. "Why do you hang around?"

These were the opening lines of Suedehead, a song we'd heard Morrissey open so many concerts with over the summer on the US tour. It was a song addressed to a lover who had become a pest, whose phone calls and silly notes had become an annoyance.

It was surely no accident that he'd chosen to open his shows with a song that posed such a pointed question, especially for those of us who came back over and over again:

Why do you come here?

Why were Nora and I following this tour? Why did we keep hanging around?

It had begun for me with the creative inspiration he'd provided as I'd found my feet as a musician. It had begun for Nora with the comfort she'd found in Morrissey's music when her mother had died.

"I'm so sorry," Morrissey sang, and everyone around us sang along and punched the air on every word. "I'm! so! sorry! sorry! oh! oh!"

But it continued because of this. Because Morrissey kept turning up and being the delightful person that he was. Because he was wildly talented and intelligent. Because he was handsome and witty. But above all else, because he kept turning his heart inside-out for all of us to see. He was so viscerally and visibly present with us, it was mesmerizing. I settled back to watch, waiting to see what this contact with the heart would reveal this time.

Morrissey was roaming the stage, and every now and then, he tossed the microphone cord around to emphasize a line. Whenever he came forward towards the edge of the stage, hands reached up towards him, hoping for a handshake.

After Suedehead came Alma Matters. It was clearly a huge favorite, big cheers greeted the opening chords.

"So, the life I have made," Morrissey sang, "may seem strange to you. But who asked you anyway? It's my life to wreck my own way."

I hadn't really gotten Alma Matters when I'd heard it first. Sure, the verse was pretty clear, but it was followed by a chorus that I found puzzling. What was it about? Loving your alma mater? Being enthusiastic about the school you attended?

"So to someone, somewhere, oh yes," Morrissey sang, the voices all around me rising with him. "Alma matters in mind, body and soul, in part and in whole."

What I hadn't understood was that this song really didn't hang together from an English-language perspective. But here in South America, it made complete sense. 'Alma' was the Spanish for 'soul'. Looked at from that angle, it became a song about living one's choices with conviction, being true to the soul.

It was a very deep sentiment that clearly struck a chord with the fans around us.

Next up was Speedway, a dramatic song about betrayal and loyalty.

"And when you slam down the hammer," Morrissey sang. "Can you see it in your heart? Can you delve so low?"

I was especially curious how this song would be received in South America. All through the US tour, right before the last verse, the lights had gone down and in the dark, the band had done a quick instrument swap, Boz Boorer who usually played guitar now on the drums, Matt Walker who played drums, now on the bass. The most notable change was that Morrissey didn't sing the last verse. His place was taken by keyboardist Gustavo Manzur, who sang the remainder of the song in Spanish.

I was curious if this audience would be excited to hear a piece of a beloved Morrissey song in Spanish. I was also curious to see how Gustavo would be received. He was from the US, but his mother was Ecuadorian, so in a sense, he was playing to his hometown audience.

"Y las mentiras, las escritas, retorcidas," Gustavo sang. "Pues no fueron, no fueron, mentiras." All those lies, written lies, twisted lies. Well, they weren't lies, they weren't lies, they weren't lies.

As he sang, there were some cheers of Gustavo! Gustavo! But at least where I stood, the audience didn't seem particularly wowed by the Spanish angle. Trinity was standing beside a local fan who erupted in indignation when Gustavo started to sing, and held up her hand, giving him the finger.

"What is this?!" she cried. "What is this?!"

"Um, Spanish?" Trinity giggled, pulling the girl's hand down in an attempt to stop her appalling gesture.

"He's ruining the ending to my favorite Morrissey song!" the girl wailed.

It was all light-hearted fun, but underscored something that proved to be true of all the fans we were to meet throughout South America. They didn't want Morrissey to try to adapt to them. They didn't need him to speak to them in Spanish. They loved him exactly as he was, and were willing to do all the leg-work—up to and including learning English for the sole purpose of understanding what he was saying in his songs. Morrissey was that kind of artist, he evoked extreme love and loyalty in his fans.

This loyalty made complete sense to me. His presence was so powerful, I could feel it working me already. Morrissey, just by walking around, singing, being himself, was playing the role of catalyst of heart experiences. The pilgrimage into the heart space had begun.

The past month of preparation for the trip had felt like one long, dry, dreary calculation. How many nights in Santiago? How many minutes to the airport? How many pesos to the dollar? How many pairs of socks? Endless, numbing mental arithmetic.

But now here was the delicacy of the heart space, the bubbling up of feeling from the depth, spring cracking the winter ice. Need I even point out that the opening of the heart can sometimes be a painful process? But it was here, it was what I had come for, it couldn't be stopped.

Not that I wanted it to. Morrissey sang song after beautiful song. Each one crowbarred my chest open just that little bit more, letting my heart breathe, letting the beauty in, letting the feelings out.

"I entered nothing, and nothing entered me," Morrissey sang, "Till you came with the key and you did your best but, as I live and breathe, you have killed me. You have killed me."

The heart is the place of contact. Things come in and touch us, we're moved, slain by them at times. It's also the place from which we reach out into the world. It's where we feel longing. Longing to be seen, to be heard, to make true meaningful connection.

Earlier in the show, Morrissey had shaken hands with Trinity and Chayane and so endearingly had explained to the crowd who they were: "Mi amigos."

I felt so happy for them, to be acknowledged so sweetly. But at the same time, I was overcome by a dreadful longing. I wanted to be one of his amigos too.

I tried for a while to talk myself out of it. Trinity and Chayane had been to hundreds of shows compared to my paltry dozens. They deserved to be acknowledged, and who knew, it might happen for me one day too. And wasn't it true that it had already happened? On the US tour? He'd shaken my hand. Twice. He'd accepted some of my writing I'd offered to him as a gift during a show. Why did I have to want more? It didn't make any sense.

And yet it was how I felt.

One of the toughest challenges of working with the heart was practicing acceptance. To just be with whatever came up, and not try to argue it away. I stood there at the barrier, looking up at Morrissey as he sang Oboe Concerto.

"The older generation have tried, sighed and died."

My heart was crowbarred open, longing for him to reach down and take my hand. It wasn't happening, he wasn't shaking my hand. It was something that might never happen, and still I stayed open and didn't shut down my heart.

How could I when Morrissey was standing singing in front of me, his heart open wide for all to see?

And then! The opening strains of Now My Heart Is Full. There was nothing to do but surrender completely to the beauty of it. A song that could hold everything my heart could possibly carry into it, the sweetness, the beauty, the pain, the longing.

That soaring chorus, "Tell all of my friends, I don't have too many, just some rain-coated lovers' puny brothers..."

Oh the exquisite agony of it. How could we bear all of these emotions, this crazy thing called being alive? Only because of songs like this. The unbearable made bearable by Morrissey opening his heart and singing.

"And I just can't explain...so...so...so..."

He came to the end of the song, and putting away his microphone, he looked over in my direction. Pausing to shake someone else's hand along the way, he walked to the spot on the stage directly in front of me, his heart still full, it was written all over him. He reached down and took my hand to shake it.

I grabbed on with my other hand, not letting go, and looking up into his eyes, said that only thing that could possibly make sense at a moment like that.

"I love you."

He didn't break contact and I took a breath and spoke again.

"I love you."

His blue eyes were looking straight into mine. The moment seemed eternal. Another breath.

"I love you."

If a security guard hadn't intervened at that point and reached up to break our clasp, I would probably still be standing there, holding his hand in both of mine, breathing, looking into his eyes, saying the only thing that made sense.

He moved on and shook more hands, then doubled back to shake Nora's. I didn't hear her speak, but she told me later that she did. She said, "I love you."

The show moved on, the end coming closer. What She Said was the last song, and the energy of it and the encore The Queen Is Dead were enlivening and electrifying, even as they made me feel the inevitability of endings. Here was the first of the 12 shows drawing to a close. The tour would be over in the blink of an eye, all of it turned to dust, meaningless, unless the heart broke through the ice to find its way into the true space of authentic connection.

We left the theater and talked a little bit with Alyssa, Chayane and Trinity, but I was rattled by the intensity of the show and we didn't linger long. Nora and I still had a couple of days in Quito before moving on, and it seemed that everything we did was colored by the space of the opening heart. I found myself taking in experiences more fully, even risky ones that spelled danger, like the speeding taxi driver who drove like he had a death wish and then tried to charge us four times the normal fare for the trip. Or the teleferico cable car ride to the top of the mountain where the effect of the sudden rise in altitude made my hands and feet tingle and throat clench and it crossed my mind that I literally was going to die from lack of oxygen.

My self-preservation self was habitually poised to panic, but really what could be done except accept the reality of what was? There was no action that could be taken in a closed cable car. My heart stayed open, held the fear, and by the time we were at the top, it was clear that I wasn't dead and so that was that. Twenty minutes sitting and breathing the thinner air, and my body adjusted and I was ready to walk around and take in the view.

And what a view! The mountains of Quito carpeted in green. The city lying between them, twinkling in the sun like someone had taken a giant bucket of glitter and spilled it out into the valley floor.

Looking at the city from this height, I pondered the mystery of how completely I felt I loved Quito even though I had sampled such tiny pockets of it. The historical district with the peaceful energy that seemed to rise up through the cobblestones and inhabit the very people. The beautiful pre-Incan statues I'd seen at the museum, so simple and precise, yet endlessly friendly and expressive. The nearby cloud forest we'd visited where we'd seen hummingbirds of infinite color hovering around a feeder, unbelievable iridescence and speedy grace.

And the wonderful afternoon we'd spent with a new friend Michael, an American anthropologist who had been forced to move to Quito with his Ecuadorian husband years ago because the federal government of the United States refused to

acknowledge their marriage, dooming
his husband to undocumented status in
the U.S. Even though they were no longer
together, Michael had stayed because he
loved Quito so much.

He had taken us out of the historical
district and brought us to a brand new
Chinese restaurant with great vegan options and to a great big mall where we
walked around looking at the high-end
stores and young people eager to see and
be seen in their trendy up-to-date clothes
and purses. Michael's friend Pablo who had lived for a while in
New York City joined us and we talked about how far gay rights
had come in Quito, how awful the government was, how scary
global corporations like Amazon.com were, and how complex
and layered the racial and social makeup of Ecuador was.

At the time when he talked about it, I felt that I could hardly
keep up with what he was saying, but sitting at the top of the
mountain, I felt that an image a tour guide had presented at a
museum we'd visited held it all. She'd talked about how in the
past, there had always been tribes that lived in the mountains
and tribes that had lived by the sea. And the fact that the tribes
that lived in the mountains used seashells as their currency was
a reminder that there was always commerce, always trade and
communication between the people who lived in very different
parts of Ecuador, under very different conditions.

Ecuador wasn't a country of opposites, each issue simplified
down into some kind of polarization: black vs white, Democrat
vs Republican, rich vs poor. It was a society of different layers,
each existing at different altitudes in different microclimates,
each with something different to offer, some with a history that
went back to the Incas and beyond, others with vigorous new

roots in our contemporary global world. It was like the side of a beautiful mountain, where Nora and I had landed and gotten to take in just a few quick tastes of the layers here and there. I hoped that one day we would get to return and taste some more.

As we walked around to take in a different vista, we were stopped by a German tourist who pointed to Nora's sweatshirt.

"I had a dream about him last night," she said. "Morrissey. The place he was playing a concert was right by my hotel and I dreamed that I wanted to go and I was trying to convince my friends to come with me."

"You should have gone," I said. "It was a great show."

"I don't even know his music," she said, laughing.

I immediately tried to rectify the situation by singing the opening lines of Suedehead to her, but it was a little bit difficult as there was a pan-pipe-and-guitar combo nearby performing that overplayed song El Condor Pasa. By matching the tempo, I was able to keep singing and must have gotten something across as her friend nodded and smiled in recognition.

"The Smiths!"

We chatted for a little while and the pan pipes stopped and I was able to serenade this woman properly with Heaven Knows I'm Miserable Now, complete with Smiths-era-Morrissey swooning and gesturing. She was utterly tickled and said she would look up his music when she got home.

As we walked away, I turned to Nora and said, "I feel like we're ambassadors from the land of Morrissey."

"Totally," she said. "And it's a good thing you can sing, cause I'm not going to!"

All too soon, it was our last night in Quito, and as we packed our bags along to the sound of El Condor Pasa floating up from the restaurant below, Nora showed me pictures that some fans had posted on Facebook: Morrissey signing autographs outside of his hotel in Quito. He was staying at the Swissotel.

"Oh!" I said. "Duh! That's why those guys were standing around in the lobby listening to Suede-head! They were waiting for him!"

It was a bit of a wrench to leave Quito, but we couldn't stay there forever, we had so many more places to visit. On the plane, I looked and looked out the window until the beautiful mountains were out of sight.

After a little while, I turned to Nora and said, "High five! We made it out of Ecuador without getting kidnapped or contracting some kind of horrible illness!"

But Nora just leaned wanly against the headrest and closed her eyes.

"Don't speak too soon," she said. "I don't feel so good."

Oh no!

NOVEMBER 11, 2015
MOVISTAR ARENA
SANTIAGO, CHILE

Nora was sick. I was out on the streets of Santiago alone. We'd checked into the hotel and Nora had gotten into bed and fallen into a dead sleep. The hotel room was not what I'd expected it to be from reading the TripAdvisor reviews. The walls were grubby, the furniture old, the safe swung open, non-functional. There was barely space to lay a suitcase down on the floor, and the bathroom was so narrow, my knees brushed against the wall when I sat on the toilet. And the WiFi didn't work. Well, it worked in tiny bursts, enough to see that our neighborhood was a vegan dead spot. Oh, and data didn't work on my phone either, not in the hotel, not anywhere in Santiago.

And now I was out on a downtown Santiago street, in the evening rush of busy professionals on their way home from work, looking for something—anything—vegan that Nora could eat.

I didn't like doing this by myself. In Quito, the currency had been the US dollar, but now I was trying to navigate purchases where the exchange rate was 700 Chilean pesos to the dollar. I felt like an idiot as cashiers twitched with irritation at my slowness, my inability to understand the simple things they said, my craning to see the numbers on the register, my attempt to hand over bills that were far too big or far too small. Chileans weren't the gentle folk of Quito. This wasn't a tourist town. There was no reason to forgive my bumbling foolishness.

I arrived back at the room with three kinds of plain rolls for Nora, along with some tea from Starbucks (I'm sorry, I don't know what kind it is, I couldn't understand what she was saying) and a cheese empanada for me (luckily, heated up, the woman behind the counter had uttered a long sentence where I'd only caught one word, caliente, which I knew meant hot. Sí! Caliente!)

Nora ate for a little while in silence, then lay back down on the pillow.

"I will now tell you how things are," she said. "I talked to my mom."

"When?" I asked, confused. Nora's mom had been dead for two years now.

"Just now," she said. Then when she saw my expression she added, "I mean, not actually, obviously! Just in my head."

This was serious. Nora was a very literal-minded person who did not sit around having regular chats with dead people.

"She told me, Oh no, I'm dead, so you must be delirious. Take your temperature. You have to let Áine take care of you. Put a wet washcloth on your head."

I put my hand on Nora's forehead. She was burning up.

"Then she told the story," Nora continued, "of the time when she was traveling in Italy and she got sick and the doctor gave her a pill, and she didn't want to take it because she had no idea what it was, but she took it. And he told her to drink lots of liquids, 'Calde, calde!' Which of course she thought meant 'cold'. This really happened, I'm not making it up. She told me a long time ago."

I got the wet washcloth for Nora's head, then told her I was going to go out and buy a thermometer so we could see how high her fever was.

"You don't have to go out again," she said. "It's pointless. I never actually have a temperature."

"Listen!" I said. "Your dead mother said I had to take care of you! So I'm going to go to a farmacia that's two blocks from here, and you're not going to give me any trouble over it, okay?"

"Okay," she said.

"I'll be back in a minute."

The farmacia turned out to be a farmacia-slash-sex-toy-shop. I wasn't going to go perusing the aisles looking for a thermometer, so I walked straight up to an old man sitting on a stool near the back and asked him if he spoke English.

"No," he said, and turned away.

"Thermometer?" I persisted. "Thermometer?"

He just shrugged.

There was one other person in the store, a woman standing behind a nearby counter. "Thermometer?" I asked her. "Thermometer?"

It clearly meant nothing to her.

Well Nora was sick and her dead mother had told me to take care of her, and I wasn't going to leave this goddamn farmacia-slash-sex-toy-shop without a thermometer in my hand.

I made eye contact with the man, held up my index finger, shook it down and then placed it under my tongue. Clearly, my finger was a thermometer.

He half-heartedly pointed to some toothbrushes.

"No," I said, then put my finger under my tongue again and put my hand to my fevered brow. "Caliente!"

"Limón?" the woman hazarded after a long pause.

"No," I said, then took my finger out of my mouth and pointed to it. This was what I needed, the freaking thermometer, not a vitamin C drink.

It was like an awful game of charades where you're stuck with teammates who have zero imagination and are just phoning it in until the buzzer goes.

Forgetting that data wasn't working in this benighted city, I took out my phone and typed 'thermometer' into Google translate. Nothing happened. Still, I showed it to the woman.

Instant understanding crossed her face.

"Oh, termómetro," she said, and turned around and fetched me a digital thermometer.

Of course, there had to be a complex interaction where she wrote me a receipt that I had to take to the man who was the cashier before I could return to her to fetch the actual thermometer and leave the store.

Back in the room, I put it in Nora's mouth and taking the meaningless reading in Celcius and putting it through a moment of WiFi on the iPad, came back with the shocking news that she had a fever of 102.

"But I never have a temperature," Nora said. "No matter how I feel, it always turns out to be 97.2. I must be really sick."

I looked at her face. Did it look kind of yellow? Oh God, what if something was terribly wrong? What if she had yellow fever? The guidebook said that if you were traveling in South America, it was a good idea to get yellow fever shots, but since they weren't mandatory anymore, I'd decided we could skip them.

And what was the prognosis for yellow fever? Death?

WiFi was only capable of intermittently loading the simplest of pages, so I couldn't call up WebMD. But I was able to load a text-only page that explained what to do in case of fever. "A fever under 100 is nothing to worry about and can be treated at home. A fever under 103 is nothing to worry about UNLESS you have recently traveled to a foreign country. In that case, make an appointment to see your doctor."

Oh God, we'd been to the cloud forest in Quito. Was a cloud forest the same as a jungle? We'd definitely been bitten by mosquitos. Was yellow fever spread by mosquitos?

"Everything is fine," I said to Nora. "You'll be fine. But I don't think you're going to make it to the show tomorrow."

A single tear escaped from her eye and slid onto the pillow.

"Okay," she said. "But you should go. I don't want to feel like I'm holding you back."

Holding me back? Who cared about the show? All that mattered was Nora, making sure that she didn't die of yellow fever on my watch. If her temperature was over 100 in the morning, I was ready to make as much of an idiot of myself as was necessary to get my message across. Pantomime, charades, my non-existent Spanish. Mi esposa! Caliente amarillo! Doctoro acqui!

In the morning, I woke up, and seeing that Nora was awake, put the thermometer in her mouth. When it beeped, I translated the reading into Farenheit.

Oh! A miracle! Nora's temperature was 99 degrees.

"How do you feel?" I asked.

"A lot better," she said. "But tired. You should go get on line. There's nothing you can do here. Really, go. I'm just going to sleep all day."

She talked a little bit about maybe coming to the show later on if she felt better, but it sounded extremely ambitious. She looked absolutely beat and she hadn't even gotten out of bed. I set her up with more bread and tea and water and Advil and charcoal capsules for her upset tummy. I left a phone on the bedside table so she could text me.

And I was off to go get on line, my heart feeling light and free. Nora was on the road to mend. I was going to get to go see Morrissey. Such a turnaround from the darkness of the night before.

I arrived at the line at 11am, a lot later than I would have planned it. We'd had an easy beginning to the tour in Quito with our seated theater show, no need to wait on line. But here in Santiago, the real work of waiting began. This show was taking place in a big venue called Movistar Arena. Thousands of people had general admission tickets to the standing floor. Getting a front-row spot at this show tonight meant getting on line early in the morning to beat the crowd, but by the looks of things, I had missed my chance, the early-bird crowd had already assembled.

I found Alyssa, she was sitting with some new pals she'd made on line, and she explained to me that there wasn't a list.

This was a surprise. At all of the general admission Morrissey shows I'd been to, there had been a list. One of the first fans to arrive on the line would administer it, they would make sure that everyone who arrived was written down in a numbered list in the order in which they arrived. This meant that people could take bathroom or meal breaks during the day, move around, mingle with their friends. Then, when it was time for doors, the administrator of the list would call out each name one by one, and the line would reform in the order in which people arrived. It was done at Morrissey shows all over the world, but apparently not in Santiago.

"There's a guy with a marker who'll write a number on your hand," Alyssa said. She showed me hers, it said B3. There were five little gates A through E, that we were all sitting in front of, and when I got my number, it was E20, which meant that I was the hundredth person to arrive.

"Is our version of the list," the guy with the marker said as he wrote on my hand.

Hundredth on line wasn't horrible. I would still end up close to the front, maybe in the third or fourth row. And really, what did I have to complain about? I was here, ready to go to the show, not stuck in bed sick like Nora. Everything was good.

It wasn't even lunchtime yet, there was a long day of waiting ahead of us. Figuring we'd all line up officially closer to doors, I went and sat with Alyssa and her new pals.

God they were smart. They spoke flawless, barely-accented English, and one of them, Diego, a 21-year-old student, had an intense conversation with Alyssa about whether it was fair to be disappointed in someone who abandoned a straight-edge life-style versus someone who abandoned veganism. I had never been straight-edge or vegan, so I just sat back and enjoyed the exchange, and thought about what it meant to be a South American Morrissey fan.

Morrissey's lyrics were so clever and nuanced, it was work enough for us native English speakers to tease out the meaning of some of his songs. What kind of effort did it take to do that in a foreign language? How far had these young people reached to make a connection with Morrissey's message? The brainpower and Morrissey-devotion around me was a tangible buzz in the air. It felt exciting. And it felt good to be around Chileans who didn't think me some kind of half-wit. A lot of these fans spoke English, and I was able to hold my own in all the conversations I got into, given the advantage of speaking my native tongue.

My favorite exchange was with a young woman called Ana. She approached me and Alyssa, asking for advice on the wording of a message in English she was printing on a Chilean flag. She came back a few minutes later to offer us a cigarette. Alyssa accepted, and we invited Ana to sit for a minute. She spoke English with a pronounced English accent, littering her speech with 'bloody' this and 'bloody' that. She was highly en-tertaining. She said something about the arena we were sitting outside of, uttering my beloved word, 'Movistar.' But she didn't say it at all like I did.

"Oh please," I said. "Say it again."

She did.

"Moh-vih-estar," I attempted.

"No," she said. "Like this."

She coached me for a minute or two, but I don't think I will ever be able to say it like a true Chilean.

The day wore on and the sun beat down. The ground was dry and dusty. There was not a scrap of shade. I had brought along an umbrella, so I opened it up and sat under it and did what I always do to pass the time in Morrissey queues.

I meditated.

Meditation was something I found quite easy to do. I was a veteran of several multi-day silent meditation retreats, so spending a few hours on line doing breath awareness or loving kindness was no kind of hardship. In fact, it was a bit of a lifesaver. Morrissey queues could sometimes be stressful. Spending ten or twelve hours stuck in one spot on an uncomfortable patch of cement with nothing to do, well, it was the kind of thing that could drive a person mad. But looked at another way, this kind of austerity, coupled with large chunks of empty time, were really quite ideal conditions under which to meditate. And the payoff was really wonderful. Instead of arriving at doors worn out and frazzled, if I filled the day with meditation, I was left emotionally balanced and mentally refreshed. Perfectly prepared to take in the wonder of another Morrissey show.

Time passed, another hour in the noonday heat. Alyssa reappeared after an epic search for the nearest bathroom. She pulled up a towel and we sat together under my umbrella, hiding from the sun. I asked her about her early days of Morrissey fandom, and she talked about seeing him at shows and festivals in California, and what it had been like to take the big leap and follow Morrissey's 2012 tour of Japan. She'd been just 21 years old. She hadn't looked back since.

It amazed me, how together she was, how she pulled all this off at such a young age. I asked her what she'd been like as a teenager. It didn't surprise me to hear that she'd been serious, studious, determined to get out of Stockton, the rough California town she'd grown up in.

"I didn't drink, I didn't party," she said. "I was like that in college too. Here we were in college in New York City, and all my friends were cutting class, having a good time, and I was like, why are you wasting this opportunity? You are here to get an education, not flunk out."

We talked about the kinds of things that motivate people, how crazy hard you'll work once you find the thing that really drives you, the thing that matters most to the innermost core of your heart.

"I found it three years ago," she said, nodding towards the arena, and the man that we would see later inside. "I've barely missed a show since. This is my life. This is what matters."

There was a period of quiet and I did my loving kindness meditation towards Morrissey, the band, the crew, each of the people I could see standing around me on line, the stray dogs that came by looking for scraps, the vendors selling vegan

sandwiches and really classy merch. I bought a Meat Is Murder patch for the back of my jacket, black rubber Morrissey bracelets, one for me and one for Nora.

And then! A flurry of texts from Nora. She had taken a little walk down to Starbucks to test her strength. She was feeling better, well enough to come to the show and stand in the back, leaning against the wall. She was in a taxi, on her way, she would be here soon.

I had picked up our tickets and with the time for doors approaching, people were standing, lining up in front of the five gates A through E. I stood with Alyssa and Diego and waited for the moment when the guy with the marker would come along and sort us according to the numbers on our hands, putting me way back, one hundredth in line. But in the meantime, Nora arrived!

She slid in beside us, I gave her an enormous hug and her ticket.

"The taxi driver was fun," she said. "Chileans don't say 'Movistar' the way we say it."

"I know!" I said.

Nora sat down on the dusty ground beside us, conserving energy. Who knew how far back she would end up when the sorting happened? The line was mammoth now. But since she was aiming for the support of the back wall, it didn't matter. But then as the minutes to doors ticked down, I had the dawning realization that there wouldn't be a sorting. The guy with the marker wasn't going to come around and demand to see the numbers on our hands and put us in our places. This was it.

I looked at where I was situated. Not only had I inadvertently gotten myself a spot third in line when I had arrived hours after some of the people standing behind me, I'd pulled Nora into the space behind me, a place she had no right to be, arriving 30 minutes before doors. And so, barring some kind of freakish mishap, Nora wasn't going to see the show leaning against the back wall, she was going to see it in the front row, propped up by the barrier.

And that was exactly what happened. The gates opened, bags quickly searched, tickets presented, and we all ran like hell, everyone vying for the best spot on the barrier. It was always like this at Morrissey shows. In the United States, venues were safety conscious, injury-lawsuit shy, and were constantly yelling at us, "No running! It's not safe!" But Chilean security didn't seem to care. The initial pack thinned out, Alyssa was soon a dot way off in front of me, disappearing through the door of the venue, and I ran on alone.

I ran, I think, literally for miles. The venue was immense. Minutes passed before I even got inside the building, and then there were minutes and minutes of going down stairs, running along a hallway, crossing a lobby. By the time I got to the entrance of the actual floor of the arena, my knees had turned to jelly and were starting to rebel. Young speedy Chileans were passing me. I was losing ground.

Don't stop! I told my body. Keep going! For Morrissey! For Nora! Run, run, run!

And I somehow found the energy to cross the giant floor, and fetched up on the barrier beside Alyssa and Diego.

"Help me!" I gasped to Diego who stood to my right. "Help me save a space for my wife!"

We stuck out our elbows and I sucked in painful gasps through my burning lungs, and far too soon, really, Nora arrived, holding her shoe in her hand, and slid into the space between me and Diego.

"Did you run?!" I said.

"Of course."

"You're nuts," I said. "You're sick."

She just shrugged.

"What's with the shoe?" I asked.

"Someone stood on the back of it," she said. "It came right off. Before the stairs, way back. I just picked it up and ran with it."

"I fell down the stairs on my ass," said Alyssa, who stood on the other side of Diego. "But in a good way—I got to the bottom really fast."

We leaned on the barrier and were quiet for a while, breathing, recovering, taking in where we were. It felt miraculous. Last night, Nora was dying of yellow fever; tonight she was not only well and alive, she was here at the show with me. And we were on the barrier! Without even trying! It felt like such a gift.

"We are so lucky," I said to Nora, taking her hand.

Later, Nora floated the theory that our 'luck' was less of a miraculous gift and more a case of us taking advantage of white privilege and Americana privilege. This was maybe the case, but at the time, I just felt massively, tearfully grateful, like the Universe was holding us idiotic kittens in its giant paws, taking care of us, making sure that everything turned out fine in the end.

Well, yes, but the end was still a ways off. Still over an hour until Morrissey took the stage and Nora wasn't looking so good. The adrenaline burst of the run into the arena had worn off and she looked dreadfully pale. I encouraged her to sit on the floor, and she did crouch down for a little while, but came back up again in response to a strange sound, a voice repeating, "Bebida-bebida-bebida-bebida!"

Something was happening that I'd never seen at a Morrissey show before. In the gulf between the barrier and the stage where security guards hung out, there were vendors wandering up and down with trays of drinks and snacks. I'd seen vendors pushing through the crowd at festivals before, selling beer, but never anything like this.

"This is very traditional," the man to my left explained. "We Chileans, we have heard this our whole childhood growing up at football games, this bebida-bebida! It brings us all back to those times."

"Is there water?" Nora asked.

No, the bebida man only sold sodas, and Nora didn't want to risk it as Gatorade had really bothered her tummy earlier.

She crouched down for another while, then came back up. She wasn't looking any better. She was so pale now, her lips were turning white.

"Can you ask the security guard for some water?" I asked the man on my left. "Please!"

He asked, but the guard just shrugged. He didn't have any.

"We need water!" I cried out, to no one in particular, and even as the words left my lips, I saw a vendor approach with bottles of water in a tray on his head.

But maybe it was too late. Nora's eyes were dilating. She was swaying on her feet.

"Buy me that water, quick!" I said to the man on my left, and turned to Nora. Her eyes closed. Her body relaxed. She fell back onto the woman standing behind her, who caught her gracefully under the arms and guided her gently to the floor. She sat unconscious for a moment or two, then opened her eyes and we all helped her to her feet.

There was water waiting for her, and right behind it, a medic, asking her questions in Spanish. Diego, who stood to the right of Nora, translated.

In those seconds while Diego translated, and the medic stood looking searchingly into Nora's eyes, I realized that I was a different person than I had been before this trip. The old self-preservation me would have overridden everything that sick Nora was about to say—her judgement was shot! she was barely conscious!—would have hauled her sick ass out of there in a hot second and gotten her back to bed. It was the safest thing to do.

But what was so great about being safe?

If we were worried about being safe, we had no business being on this trip, and yet here we were. Standing at the barrier with Morrissey less than an hour away, was I going to pull the plug on the whole thing? Take Nora's hand and march her out of there?

"I just needed some water," Nora said to the medic, and Diego translated. "I was dehydrated. And now that I've had some, I feel fine. I promise if I feel bad again, I'll just leave. I promise."

Searching her face deeply, like he was doing some kind of Vulcan diagnostic mind meld, the medic eventually nodded and left. She had passed the test.

I also took a good long look at Nora. Passing out seemed to have done her the world of good. The color had returned to her face, she looked alert and animated.

"I really just needed water," she said. "I really feel fine."

It was so tempting to follow the fear, make a knee-jerk decision to bundle Nora off to safety. Then no one could say it was my fault if anything went wrong. But, oh God, how many things in life had I missed by playing it safe? How many Saturday nights spent at home reading books? How many adventures passed up because they seemed too risky?

It had taken me a number of decades, but I'd finally figured out that safety was a great big trap, and Nora and I had busted out and taken the leap and gone on this adventure. But did we have the guts, the tenacity, the stamina to see it through?

I really didn't know, but in that moment, I wanted with all of my heart to try.

"Okay," I said to Nora. "We'll stay."

Having made that decision, my body relaxed. The crisis was over. The adrenaline that had been coursing through my veins drained away, and I felt my energy level dropping. But, oh! My hands and feet began to tingle, my ears started to ring, all signs that I was on my way to passing out.

Oh come on! For real? Me too? This was ridiculous!

I crouched down and took deep breaths and tried to pull myself together. My head was resting on the barrier, and on the other side of it, my eye was caught by a bottle of water. The word 'vital' was printed on the cap.

You're right, I thought. Water is vital. Did I drink any of it today? Did I eat any food?

"I need water!" I said to Nora.

"Coming right up!" she said.

Food was another matter. I couldn't eat sugar for health reasons, and all the stuff the vendors were selling were sugary snacks.

And so just because I needed him, a vendor appeared before us selling nothing but Lay's potato chips.

I tore into the giant bag and shoveled the chips into my mouth. Carbohydrates! Fat! Salt! I could feel my blood pressure rising, my energy returning. I stood up, and at that moment, the giant screen on the stage came alive and the preshow videos began. Joey Ramone grabbed the microphone. "You're a loudmouth baby, you better shut up! One! Two! Three! Four!"

I turned and grinned at Nora. Now, for real, I could feel it in my bones, we were going to make it. Everything was going to be fine.

When Morrissey took the stage, he and the band were all in white shirts; they looked fantastic. A massive cheer greeted their appearance. It was incredible to be seeing him again. There was nothing guaranteed about this; Nora and I were here tonight by the skin of our teeth, and yet it was happening. A little miracle.

"Buenos noches, Santiago!" Morrissey said and began Suede-head.

The crowd was enthusiastic and warm. Morrissey shook a lot of hands in the front row during Suedehead and Alma Matters. I was particularly happy to see him reach down and shake Diego's hand. He had been so lovely to be around all day, and had been so seamlessly helpful in translating Nora's conversation with the medic. He deserved a medal for being such a gentleman, but instead got this handshake, which I'm sure he valued much more!

Morrissey shook Alyssa's hand too, which was just so right. In Quito, he'd gotten around to Trinity and Chayane, then me and Nora. But now in shaking Alyssa's hand, he had acknowledged all of us five US fans who were going to be with him for the whole tour. It was very fitting.

Every Morrissey show is different. Each one has its own flavor, its own distinct essence. Often, Morrissey shows can be heavy emotional weather. It was certainly the case for me in Quito. The process of opening the heart can bring a lot to the surface. I can't count the number of times I've cried my eyes out at a Morrissey show.

But that wasn't the case tonight. Perhaps because my heart had been opened so thoroughly in Quito, I wasn't feeling much sturm und drang. I felt free and happy, able to simply take in the show and enjoy it to the utmost.

And there was so much to enjoy!

After Alma Matters, a picture of Bruce Lee looking very stylish appeared on the screen behind Morrissey and the band launched into the intro of a song I couldn't place. It wasn't anything they'd played in Quito, nothing I recognized from the US tour. What could it be?

Then a second before Morrissey started singing, recognition dawned. Oh my God! It was This Charming Man!

"Punctured bicycle on a hillside desolate," Morrissey sang. "Will nature make a man of me yet?"

The crowd went wild, everyone jumping up and down, singing along. And why shouldn't they? This Charming Man was a blast. It was one of Morrissey's earliest hits with the Smiths and over thirty years later, it still stood out as being one of the best songs he'd ever written.

The song was about an exchange between a young man who has abandoned his punctured bicycle and an older man who picks him up in his "charming car" where "the leather runs smooth on the passenger seat." But I noticed that tonight, Morrissey, noted animal rights activist that he was, changed the word "leather" to "pleather." It was a nice touch.

"I would go out tonight," Morrissey sang, "But I haven't got a stitch to wear!"

It was the best line in the song and we all wailed along with total abandon. What fun! And really, it was clear that we fans weren't the only ones who were really getting a kick out of this song. The band were throwing themselves into it—they'd given it a different twist from the original Johnny Marr jangle pop sound from years ago. Today's Charming Man had grown up, and now had a solid, thumping beat that, especially during the "jumped up pantry boy" section, truly rocked. Oh my God, it was bliss!

The show went on, Morrissey, light and happy, expressive in his gestures. At times, when he moved in a certain way, or when he was backlit by the strong stage lights, I saw a much younger Morrissey, a Smiths-era Morrissey in his silhouette.

"I loff you!" he said after more than one song, and often, "Gracias!"

There was also a playful moment after one song where he said, "So, as I think you know, we cannot find a record deal in England, we cannot find a record deal in the USA, and so, we are moving to Chile!"

This news was received with great enthusiasm from the crowd, naturally!

Everything about the show was so fantastic, to be eaten up with a spoon. The setlist was different from the Quito show—no two Morrissey shows were ever the same—and tonight we had the addition of an Elvis cover, a song called You'll Be Gone that suited Morrissey's voice so completely. This was a case of a cover version of a song sounding so much better than the original. Elvis's treatment of the song made syrupy mush of the sweet lyrics, "Your lips pressed to mine, is Heaven descending, and I could die because it is ending." But in Morrissey's hands, it came clearly across as a genuine plea for a moment of intimacy to never end.

He sounded authentic as he sang this song—and all of his own songs—not because he "did authentic" well. In Morrissey, the authenticity of his connection to his heart was what came first. The songs were then vehicles to express what was in his heart, and so every time we heard them, each song was differently nuanced, completely unique, rich with meaning.

It was true that the setlist was always different, but there was also a certain pattern that the show followed. Before long, we got to the point of the show where everything went quiet and Gustavo played a gorgeous, expressive solo piece on the piano. It wasn't an introduction that was tied to any specific song, but rather a signal that one of Morrissey's more emotional songs was about to start.

"My Dearest Love," the man on my left guessed.

"Yes, I Am Blind," I responded.

"Will Never Marry," he countered.

We waited and the band played the opening chord of the song.

"Yes!" the man beside me said. "Will Never Marry!"

Morrissey stepped closer to the microphone and sang, "I'm writing this to say, in a gentle way, thank you but no."

"Aw! Yes!" a woman standing behind me shouted in the pause before the next line. "Yes!" I shouted, joining her.

Morrissey gave us a look out of the side of his eye. I couldn't be sure, but I got the feeling that he was suppressing a smile.

"I will live my life as I will undoubtedly die—alone!"

"You'll have us!" the woman shouted.

"True!" he conceded, and the whole band came in, and he sang the whole beautiful rest of the song without any more interruption from us.

Song after song, so wonderfully executed. Everything that Morrissey sang, everything that the band played was done with such precision and zest, it was a joy to listen to. After Will Never Marry, Morrissey paused for introductions.

"I am very pleased to have muchachos with cojones," he said, and named each member of the band, starting on the right with Gustavo Manzur on the keyboard, then Jesse Tobias lead guitarist, Matt Walker on drums, then newest addition to the band, Mando Lopez on bass, and finally the most longstanding member of Morrissey's band, and the one who always got the biggest cheer, guitarist, Boz Boorer, or as Morrissey put it, "tra la la la, Boz Boorer."

Over the last year, I'd seen this particular iteration of Morrissey's band play a lot of shows. It was really very easy to believe that they were the best band that Morrissey had ever assembled. Each member of the band sounded exactly right, and they came together in a tight harmonious unit that brought an extra amazingness to every single song. I preferred the live version that these guys did of every song I heard them play. It was a part of the thrill of seeing Morrissey live, getting to experience how these songs evolved and grew, not just through Morrissey's vocal interpretation of them—which was always fresh and fascinating—but through the richness of the band's take on them.

But what I really couldn't believe—yet I had to because I was experiencing it firsthand—was the fact that this magnificent band at the top of its game just kept outshining itself. These shows in South America were better than anything we'd seen in the US or Europe. How was this possible? Some of those shows were the best I could possibly imagine a Morrissey show to be, and yet, here were the band being better than the best. And along with them, here was Morrissey's heart, infusing each word of each song with the most delicious depth of meaning.

For the last song, Morrissey sang the wistful and wonderful Everyday Is Like Sunday. Sometimes this song was heart-rendingly bleak, but tonight it was light and lovely, particularly pleasing, especially with Morrissey getting down on his knees for the line "Come Armageddon!"

And then, un-believably, the show was over! Morrissey said, "I love you!" and left the stage. Where had the time gone? Nora and I looked around us and, our hearts overflowing with gratitude, offered our places on the barrier to the two women standing behind us so that they could be at the front for the encore.

"Why?" the petite Will-Never-Marry heckler asked.

The question completely stumped me. Didn't she want her time at the barrier, a chance for a handshake?

"Because you love Morrissey," Nora said, and this seemed to satisfy her. She slipped in front of me, and Morrissey came back in a brown shirt, took a bow with the band and made the joke, "Thank you for listening—if you did!" before launching into What She Said.

This was another classic from the Smiths, a brash and cheerful uptempo song, but of course, in true Morrissey style, the words were utter misery.

"What she said," Morrissey began, "How come someone hasn't noticed that I'm dead and decided to bury me, God knows I'm ready."

Dark, dark lyrics, but in even truer Morrissey style, he stood on the stage and was able to infuse them with the lightness and humor of the night, without losing any of the meaning.

"What she said," he sang at the end of the song, "I smoke because I'm hoping for an early death and I need to cling to something."

As he sang the word "cling" he reached out and grasped a bunch of sunflowers that someone in the front row had been offering to him all night. The line was repeated, and on the second "cling" someone handed him a Chilean flag that he could cling to. He clung to the flag as he sang the outro from Rubber

Ring that the song segues into, a haunting vocal piece that ended the show so beautifully.

"Hasta luego!" he said, ripped off his shirt, threw it into the crowd and, pausing for a moment as Matt Walker kicked over his drum kit, left the stage and it was all done.

Oh! I looked at Nora and she was glowing, her face shining, mirroring what I felt, amazed by the incredibleness of the show we had seen. There was nothing to say. No question. It had been worth everything—yellow fever, sickness, passing out, every-thing—to be here. Our days of staying safe at home avoiding all risks were firmly over. We were on this adventure, we were in it all the way, we were ready to take it as far as it would go.

NOVEMBER 14, 2015
PRIMAVERA FAUNA
SANTIAGO, CHILE

We weren't done with Chile yet. There was a second gig in Santiago, a festival that Morrissey was headlining called Primavera Fauna. Nora and I took it quite easy during the two days off before the festival. She was wiped out, exhausted, and since I had a bit more get-up-and-go, I went out to check out the pre-Columbian museum in Santiago to see if they had anything interesting. The pre-Columbian museum in Quito'd had some amazing stuff, pre-Incan pieces that echoed the Ancient Egyp-

tian aesthetic I loved so much. But here in Santiago, no luck, their collection didn't stretch back far enough in time to ring those pre-Incan bells.

There was this one gem, though. A larger-than-life-sized statue that was unmistakably a representation of Morrissey. I wondered when he'd traveled back in time to pose for this one. Looked like some time in the early 90s.

On our last free day in Santiago, we made an effort and caught a subway out to the Barrio Italia, so that we could eat something a bit more interesting than french fries or crackers for dinner. We sat on the patio of a coffee shop as we waited for the nearby vegan restaurant Shakti to open for dinner, and watched a startling number of people walk by wearing t-shirts bearing the names of classic bands. Kiss, REM, AC/DC, even the Smiths! The woman was gone before I had the thought to call out "nice shirt!"

Dinner was magnificent. It was amazing how good food could completely change your opinion of a city. Sure, we'd gotten off to a rocky start, but Santiago wasn't so bad after all! Nora was getting better, here were these lovely people in this lovely vegan restaurant, the chef coming out of the kitchen to chat with us in English.

I can't remember what it was that Nora asked me to look up on my phone. Something inconsequential, I never got around to it. Because when I took out my phone and looked at Facebook, there were all of these worried messages posted on fellow-Morrissey-fan Guillaume's Facebook page.

"Oh crap!" I said to Nora. "Something's happened in Paris."

The light went out of the evening. A terrorist attack. Not just one, but many. Innocent people gunned down in a theater. Dozens of people dead, the death toll mounting. In Paris! Why? What was behind this?

I didn't even want to know. It didn't even matter. It was the same story again. Some fanatics running with some crazy idea, in the grip of the awful conviction that slaughtering innocent people was the only way forward, the only solution. It was monstrous.

But Guillaume was safe, everyone we knew was safe, the attacks were over, there wasn't anything to fear. All this terror was half a world away, in Paris, oh poor beautiful Paris, and we went to bed and got up in the morning and met with Alyssa, Chayane and Trinity so that we could make our way out together to Primavera Fauna.

Morrissey was headlining the festival, he wouldn't be appearing on the main stage until 10:30pm. But we all wanted to be in the front row to see him, so that meant that we had to get to the festival before the gates opened so that we could claim our spots on the barrier before anyone else arrived, and hang onto them by staying put all day and all evening until Morrissey finally appeared.

We timed it so that we'd arrive before the first bus that was ferrying in festival-goers from the city. The venue was called Espacio Broadway, and it was a swimming pool complex in the middle of nowhere, about 30 minutes outside of Santiago. I was extremely curious to see what it was like. Back at home, I'd spent a lot of time Google mapping and translating the posts about transit options on the event's Facebook page.

The information I'd gleaned had been kind of hilarious. Because Google translated "Espacio Broadway" as "space Broadway", I kept reading posts that had preambles like, "Morrissey is appearing in space…" or "Transportation options to get to space…" The five of us ended up using the Uber option to get to space and now here we were, among the first dozen people waiting for the gates of the festival to open.

I think I am quite unusual among Morrissey fans. Pretty much every Morrissey fan I've spoken to about the topic has expressed the opinion that they really dislike festivals. I think it's pretty fair to say that Morrissey himself isn't overly fond of them. But I love them. I like planting myself in my spot, knowing at noon that this is where I'll be ten hours later when Morrissey takes the stage. I like the pace of the day. Something about the long, slow parade of mediocre bands, with Morrissey waiting at the end of it, I don't know, it just suits my temperament.

It was a beautiful day, and as I looked through the bars of the fence that we were waiting behind, I couldn't see any swimming pools, so that nixed the image of Morrissey singing to a crowd of people on a chlorine-scented concrete patio. We waited and waited and entertained ourselves by seeing if we could remember what the list of forbidden and recommended items posted beside us meant. Nora and I had painstakingly fed it all through Google translate the night before. Some were obvious, I remembered what bloquedar solar (sunblock) was, I needed tons of that. Also a gorro (hat) and anteojos de sol (sunglasses), or I'd come out a lobster at the end of the day.

"Ropas abrigadas is warm clothes," I said, and I'd brought some, though who could believe that this golden warm day could ever get cold.

No drogas was easy, but Chayane had to help us out with the weapons, knives and grilling-in-the-parking-lot portion of the rules.

"And do you know what this is?" he asked. "No mascotas?"

"Yes!" we both said.

When we'd seen it last night, we'd been so puzzled by it. What did it mean? No mascots? No giant rodent- or bear-costumed actors taking the field at half-time between bands?

"A mascota is a pet," I said. "It means 'no pets.'"

Mascota was such a wonderfully evocative word for a pet, it was now my favorite word in Spanish. I called Nora "my pet" all the time, but from now on she was going to be "mi mascota."

And then a stir at the front of the line, time for doors!

I jogged up to a free security guard and presented my bag to be searched. He looked at it like, What do you expect me to do with this?

"You don't want to search it?" I said. "You want me to take the things out?"

I mimed pulling the stuff out, and he nodded, and when I got to my paragua (umbrella), he had a long confab with the security guard beside him about whether paraguas were allowed or not. I didn't want him to confiscate it because it was an important part of my sun protection regimen, but I also wished he would hurry up and decide, so I could get to the barrier of the main stage. Just ten hours until Morrissey came on, and those spots on the barrier were filling up as the seconds ticked by.

Finally he nodded, the paragua was okay, and I ran past him to the ticket taker and then ran on into the festival grounds, Primavera Fauna, Espacio Broadway, Morrissey in space.

And who could have dreamed up a space like this? I was running through a great expanse of green, a field dotted with stages and concession stands, each decorated with light blue and green

flags that whipped merrily in the breeze, the beloved Movistar logo jumping out at me everywhere I looked. In the distance, pale blue mountains ringed the space, holding up the edges of a sky that was spilling golden sunlight onto everything, the kind of light that made me feel like I was on the set of a South American movie.

I arrived on the barrier beside Chayane and a group of his South American pals. Nora wasn't far behind me. Alyssa and Trinity were behind her, they dropped their bags beside us on the barrier, and went off to look for something to eat. Chayane left soon after them, but Nora and I placed our snowy-white hotel towels on the ground and sat where we were planted. This was our spot. This was our place. This is where we would be ten hours from now when Morrissey would appear.

Where does time go on a day like that? As always, my pre-show routine involved meditation. And there was something about the space around me that really enhanced the meditative experience. The golden sunlight, the vast expanse of blue sky, it was like the big clear space that was Espacio Broadway evoked a similar clarity and big space inside my mind. It was easy to be aware of my thoughts and feelings as they arose and subsided, everything was held lightly in awareness in this space that could hold anything.

Such beautiful empty space outside of me too!

In this emptiness, things arose and subsided, just like thoughts and feelings did inside. Alyssa and Trinity returned to deliver their report on all the vegan food options available at the festival. The crowd swelled behind us in anticipation of the appearance of the first band of the day. Nora left and reappeared with lunch.

Whole bands appeared on the stage, sang, disappeared. I was pleasantly diverted by them, amused by their antics. The lead singer of Miami Horror at one point appalled security by scaling the scaffolding beside the stage and singing his song sitting 50 feet aloft, among the blue and green fluttering flags. But nothing really left much of a mark on the golden space that held everything.

And time? It wasn't the usual heavy hammer, mechanically marking out each hour. It was a light thing, a thin gauze, easily seen through.

The third band of the day was the Cardigans, a Swedish group that had been on the radio constantly the year I graduated from college. This was back when I still lived in Ireland, and that bleak winter of 1996/97 was one of the darkest times of my life.

It should have been the best. At a very young age, I had set myself the goal of surviving my monstrous childhood. It didn't matter what happened, I told myself. One day I would leave this desolate farm in the West of Ireland, get out from under these parents and siblings who didn't give a crap about me. Yes, one day, I would be a grown-up! I would have my own money, my own flat! I would live in a big city, and I would do Whatever I Wanted!

And it happened. When I graduated from college, I got a job testing financial software in IBM's Dublin office. I had a nice flat, money. It was time to do Whatever I Wanted. Turned out, all I wanted to do was die. I could see no future, nothing to live for, just an endless march of days turning up in a beige office, doing nothing that meant anything.

Lovefool by the Cardigans was the soundtrack to that time. It was a great song. Some morn-ings, I woke up to it on my clock radio, and in those few minutes, there was respite, some moments of sunshine before the horror of my life rushed in and took me under for the rest of the day.

There was another song that played during that time. It wasn't quite a song, it was more like a message that my future self kept calling out to me. It wasn't quite in words, though. It was just a feeling/thought/ certainty, a knowing that I HAD to move to New York. That if I moved to New York everything would be fine, perfect, better than I could ever imagine. New York New York New York, better than the grave! this feeling said. Drop everything, apply for a visa. Go.

So I did. I won the Green Card lottery and within months, I packed everything I owned into two bags and crossed the Atlantic and started a new life, my real life, the one where I got to be a creative person, not a software tester, where I had all the right resources at my fingertips to undo the horrible scripts of my childhood and build healthy relationships. New York! Where the gentle, beautiful soul that was the love of my life lived, my Nora, mi mascota. New York! Better than the grave!

As I stood at the barrier and watched the lovely Cardigans performing, all of this ran through me. Except now I was looking at it from the other side. I WAS my future self, fingering the gauzy veil of time, living the magical, golden life that I'd been promised. A thought suddenly occurred to me.

"What if it wasn't a metaphor?"

I thought about this theoretical message from my future self. I'd always thought of it as some kind of hopeful, lucky guess. But what if it had actually been a real message? One that my real future self had consciously made an effort to send?

And since I now WAS that future self, what better day than this time-out-of-time day to send it.

And then, oh perfect, the Cardigans launched into Lovefool, and it was easy as anything, I connected to the song, tied a message to it, and sent it back to the past. There was nothing to it, I just transmitted the feeling I remembered receiving: New York New York New York, where everything works out better than great. Go now, get a Green Card, don't die, go to New York instead!

Was it really real? Had I just saved my own life by sending a message through time? Had it worked?

Based on results, I think definitely yes.

The Cardigans left the stage. The day was moving on. Just one more band to go before Morrissey. Nora and I sat, resting our backs against the barrier. After a little while, I heard shouts beside us of "Gustavo! Gustavo!" The Gustavo who immediately leapt to mind was Gustavo Manzur, Morrissey's keyboard player, but Morrissey's people wouldn't be setting up until later. Or would they?

I poked my head up above the barrier, and about ten feet away, there was Gustavo, standing at the barrier, chatting with some fans.

"Gustavo's here!" I said to Nora and she got up and we stood quietly waiting for him to make his way towards us down the line.

This was very exciting. We had neither of us met any of Morrissey's band, but having seen them at so many shows, we'd been blown away time after time by their musical talents. Gustavo was a phenomenon. He not only played the keyboard exquisitely, he sang the Spanish parts of the songs, played the accordion, trumpet, flamenco guitar, didgeridoo. Pretty much every time I looked at him, he was playing a different instrument. Not only that, he had written the music for some of the songs on World Peace Is None of Your Business, including one of my favorites, Earth Is the Loneliest Planet. And to top it all off, he just seemed like a really nice guy. He was basically one of my favorite people in the world I'd never met.

But that situation was about to be remedied.

He made his way to our group, and first Chayane hopped over the barrier for a bear hug and a long chat in Spanish. Then it was our turn.

I introduced myself, and was immediately enveloped in a warm hug. With my cheek pressed against his, I told him how amazing the show in Quito had been. It had been my favorite show so far of the tour, and I had a sense that it was special for him too.

"I was so nervous!" he said, laughing. "My mother was there! My biggest critic!"

He hugged Nora, Alyssa, Trinity, posed for a photo.

"How are you guys?" he asked. "You okay? Can I get you anything? Water?"

How sweet!

"Yes, please," I said. "Water would be great!"

He returned a few minutes later with bottles of water for all, and before he took off, he turned to tell us one last thing. Somehow, I really don't know how, I ended up holding his hand as he spoke.

"Show that man some love tonight," he said. "Go crazy."

"We always do," I said.

I never took my cues from fans around me. I always expressed exactly how I felt at shows, and what I felt always contained a big portion of super-goofy arm-waving exuberant delight.

"I know," Gustavo said. "But tonight make him blush!"

The sun set as the final band before Morrissey played, an instrumental group called Explosions in the Sky. The wordless music left me space to think. It got colder as it got darker. A stiff breeze was blowing and I put on my ropas abrigadas. I thought about Paris. I thought about Morrissey. I thought about what Gustavo had said, and wondered what effect the Paris attacks had had on Morrissey. Maybe they'd gotten under his skin and gotten him down.

An entertaining card appeared on the screen. The artist appearing next was spelled "Morrisey." After a few minutes, the error was corrected. Then the pre-show videos played and in no time at all, the dramatic music that heralded Morrissey's arrival on stage was playing, and there he was. It was funny to see Gustavo too, taking his place right in front of us when we'd spoken so recently. There was no eye contact, no smiles. He was all seriousness, his work face on.

Before the first song, Morrissey took the microphone.

"Tonight," he said, "we are throwing our arms around Paris!"

He launched into Suedehead, followed again by This Charming Man. The audience was delighted, and even more so by the

next song, First of the Gang. It was a super catchy song, and I looked back to see a massive sea of people, all of them singing along, bouncing up and down in time with the music.

"Thank you," Morrissey said, when the song ended. "It's our pleasure, it's our honor to be here with you."

It was a huge audience. Looking back over my shoulder, I could see the big lights from the stage illuminating the first half or three quarters of the crowd, but beyond that, there were still thousands of people, seeming to go on forever into the pitch-black night around us.

Alma Matters, Speedway, Ganglord. The stage was bright, bright, bright. The screen behind Morrissey and the band was massive, and it wasn't the usual movie-screen-and-projector set-up that they used at indoor venues. It was a backlit digital screen, and so the video montage of police brutality that played during Ganglord was disturbingly crisp and clear.

The stage was big and high, and as was often the case at festivals, there was a massive gap between the stage and the barrier behind which we stood. Here we were in the front row, and it felt like Morrissey was miles away, unreachable.

The set was superb, the massive crowd enthusiastic and responsive. And my heart ached and ached for Morrissey alone up there on stage, singing oh so sweetly, gorgeously, out into the blackness of the night. God knows I wanted to obey Gustavo's command. I would have been very happy to whoop and holler so loud, it made Morrissey blush. But I could only be myself. My hand clutched my chest for the whole show, my heart was wrung by the relentless, beautiful vulnerability Morrissey was showing. All I could see was this beautiful figure whose aloneness was utterly complete.

But was Morrissey really feeling alone? How could I tell? How much of this was him, and how much was me?

It was hard to say. One of the most wonderful things about Morrissey's presence on stage was the richness of what he could hold for—and convey to—his audience. He tapped so deeply into his own self as he sang, it evoked an answering experience of the deep self in those who heard him. He was a really powerful artist, and

the art that he showcased was the self that he revealed to us on stage. This self stood as a symbol of our own selfhood that we could all interact with, and in that process, learn more about who we really were.

Like many other Morrissey fans, I identified deeply with him. I identified with him as a singer. I identified with him as a writer. I identified with the content of his songs. I identified with the artist in him who revealed himself in such an autobiographical way. Every time I saw him, he called forth an awareness of some aspect of my self. Often, looking up at him on stage, he was simply my heart.

But tonight, in my eyes, he was the aspect of me that was utterly alone. He was isolation. A self by definition can only be a self if it is separate from others. And this separateness was all I could see, all I could feel.

"Earth is the loneliest planet of all," he sang out into the cold breeze, "Live with aloneness that no one else knows."

I felt myself, his self, all of our selves stuck on this planet, stuck in a place where people could walk into a theater and gun people down, inflicting terror and mayhem. Stuck in bodies that could wave and pass crude signals across the gulf that divided us, but did anything really get across? Life in this body on this planet was isolation complete.

I would like to say that the memory of the golden sunlight of the day reasserted itself at this point, pouring in and healing all my ills. But it didn't. Thinking about it amplified the hopelessness of the situation. What good did it do to meditate? What good did it do to transcend the ugliness of life, if that ugliness lived on as vigorously as ever, even as I floated above it? What good was golden beauty, loving kindness, Ancient Egyptian art, pre-Incan statues, if none of it actually touched anything, made any difference? If it didn't have the power to stop the mayhem, what use was it to anyone?

Separation, isolation, it was unavoidable.

Morrissey sang on to the end of the song and concluded, "And there is nothing anyone can do."

How true it was.

How Soon Is Now? You Have Killed Me.

"Now please," Morrissey said, introducing the next song, Meat Is Murder. "I beg you, por favor, por favor, I beg you, I beg you, I beg you, stop eating animals."

This was another song with graphically violent footage playing on the super-crisp video screen. This time it was images of animals being slaughtered for food, the massively barbaric practices of factory farming showed on the screen in vividly gory detail. People often averted their eyes for this one, sometimes unsuspect-

ing first-timers watched and were so overcome, they passed out. It was very strong stuff. But weirdly, Meat Is Murder was, I think, my favorite song to hear Morrissey sing live. He meant it so fervently, poured so much of himself into it, it touched me in a way I could hardly fathom every time.

"The meat in your fat fucking mouth is murder!" Morrissey sang. "No! No! No! It's murder! KFC is murder! Ah, but do you care, do you care, do you care?"

The poorness of the design of all of this was breathtakingly grim. Here was one of the most creative people alive, who had put so much of himself into the effort of fashioning these songs, these messages. He was pouring himself into singing them to us night after night, year after year, and after all of that, there was a good chance that he would go to his grave still feeling isolated, that it hadn't really worked, that there was a hole in his heart that could never be touched.

At the end of Meat Is Murder, he left the stage, and came back wearing a black jacket with gold lapels. Silence fell. Gustavo began the haunting piano solo that signaled something special. That something was Everyday Is Like Sunday.

"Trudging slowly over wet sand," Morrissey sang, "back to the bench where your clothes were stolen."

Oh God. The dreadful isolation that can never be broken, it was held alongside the sweetest connection. In the middle of the song, on the line, "a strange dust lands on your face," golden lights came on and shone out onto us, the audience. Our faces lit up like sunflowers turned to him.

"On your face," Morrissey sang, walking along the edge of the stage, looking at our faces. "On your..." then he started to giggle, half singing, half laughing along to the music. We were apparently that funny to look at. And you know what? He was pretty funny too. As epically painful as all of it was, I couldn't help smiling, laughing back at him.

In that moment, the howling pain of the black isolated mayhem, and the golden beauty shining above it all, they finally met, sewn together by the one force that trumped everything.

We loved him. We all loved him enough to turn up and open our hearts to him.

He loved us. He loved us enough to sing to us wholeheartedly, no matter what was in that heart.

The show was coming soon to a close. But there was a song that he hadn't sung yet. The screen lit up bright behind him in a tricolor, red, white and blue.

"As you know, as you've heard," he said, "the war of religion is upon us, or the religion of war is upon us, and we say, no thank you! No, no, no, no, no, no, no!"

He sang I'm Throwing My Arms Around Paris like Paris herself was on the stage with him, an invisible figure walking beside him, shot, traumatized. He cradled her in his outstretched arm as he walked back and forth, the other hand holding the microphone, singing his heart out.

And then the show was over.

"Thank you for listening," he said. "The taxi has arrived."

"No!" we protested.

"It's not my fault," he said. "You know how the meter goes, tick tick tick."

We laughed.

"Adiós," he said. "Hasta luego."

And after a rousing The Queen Is Dead, he said, "I loff you" over and over into the microphone, and left so reluctantly, it was like he was being dragged off the stage by an invisible hook.

We left, and it took the longest time to connect to Uber, to find our driver. I was so glad Chayane was with us, talking on the phone with the driver, asking questions, finding things out.

We finally got into the car, Chayane up front, Alyssa and Trinity in the middle, looking totally beat by the long festival day, and me and Nora in the back, our heads together, whispering about how amazing it had been to meet Gustavo, how incredible the show had been, how we loffed each other, loffed Morrissey, loffed this crazy life where we traveled halfway across the world to hear a man sing a song that somehow made everything make sense.

NOVEMBER 17, 2015
TEATRO RENAULT
SÃO PAULO, BRAZIL

And so we crossed a threshold. With the beginning of the tour firmly over, we made our way into Brazil. It was a massive country, comparable in size to the United States, and with just as much cultural and geographic diversity. We were spending three weeks in total in Brazil, taking in four shows in three different cities—São Paulo, Rio de Janeiro and Brasilia—then ending with a side trip to Salvador on the east coast before moving on to Paraguay.

Brazil was the only country in South America where Portuguese was spoken. I had made a reasonable effort to learn some Spanish phrases for this trip, but had balked at the idea of simultaneously learning Portuguese. On the plane from Santiago to São Paulo, I realized that I was facing into three weeks in Brazil and I literally couldn't speak a word of Portuguese. Not even 'hello' or 'thank you' or the super-crucial all-purpose phrase 'I'm sorry, I don't speak Portuguese.'

So I spent the last couple of hours before we arrived in Brazil trying to prepare myself. What was happening? Where were we going?

When it came to research, Nora was the Boss of All Brazil, and she had chosen our hotels in São Paulo. Because the city was so massively sprawling, the venues of the two shows were almost an hour's drive apart. For our last two days in São Paulo, we were staying at a chain hotel within walking distance of Citibank Hall, but for the bulk of our trip, we were staying in a hotel that wasn't too far from Teatro Renault called Hotel Unique.

As our plane drew closer to São Paulo, I took out the guidebook and flipped through São Paulo's top attractions: Ibirapuera Park, a massive park reminiscent of New York's Central Park, Batman Alley, a winding street devoted to one of São Paulo's top art forms, graffiti. And what was this? Listed under the attractions was a very familiar-sounding destination: Hotel Unique. An eye-catching modern hotel shaped like a slice of watermelon, it was so stylish and striking, it was a recommended tourist activity to go check it out, and stop for a drink at the rooftop Skye Bar.

"But wait," I said, turning to Nora. "This is where we're staying, right? Hotel Unique?"

She nodded, looking glum.

"It sounds like a seriously nice place," I said.

She nodded again. "I think it's a terrible mistake."

"Why?" I said. And then it dawned on me. "Oh."

There was an endless world of Morrissey fandom online. Websites, interviews, articles, Facebook groups, chatrooms, catalogues of every record, every lyric, the color of every shirt he'd ever worn to every show. I didn't spend any time at all on these sites. In certain respects, I was a dreadful Morrissey fan. Because I had become a fan in the age of iTunes, I didn't know which album any of my favorite songs were from. I liked the Smiths songs, I'd even gone to see Johnny Marr once, but I just couldn't get as worked up about the past as most fans did. It wasn't that I didn't care. It was just that my caring was exclusively directed towards the actual Morrissey who was currently alive now. I wanted to experience him as he was in the present, I wanted to hear the music he cared about today, not get involved in endless dead-end online discussion of the possibility of a Smiths reunion.

Nora was more connected with the online Morrissey world than I was, and so it had entered her consciousness that when Morrissey had last appeared in São Paulo, he had stayed at Hotel Unique. This was one of the reasons she had booked it, in the hopes that he'd stay there again and we'd run into him.

"This was a dreadful idea," she said. "Things here aren't at all like I pictured."

I knew what she meant. Before we'd left, she'd shown me some footage of Morrissey signing autographs for South American fans outside of his hotel. It had all been so sweet, I could see how Nora had wanted to be a part of something that just didn't happen at home or in Europe.

But in actually being here, it had become clear that these lovely scenes were happening not because Morrissey was more relaxed and available in South America, hanging out in his hotel wanting to chat. Local fans were encountering him because they were putting in some serious hours sitting in the lobby, waiting for that moment when Morrissey would emerge.

It was true that Nora and I were no strangers to waiting. We put in tons of hours waiting to get our spots on the barrier at a show. But now that we were in South America, it was clear that some things were okay for the locals to do, but not for us. Lying in wait for someone to emerge from their hotel room sounded a lot like stalking. South American fans had a very polite and deferential manner, the nicest stalkers you could ever hope to encounter. But we weren't South American fans, it was clear that this scene was very much not for us.

"But we're just guests at the hotel," I said to Nora, trying to reassure her. "If we ran into Morrissey, it would just be by accident."

"Yeah," Nora said. "Maybe we'll be lucky and he won't be there at all."

We arrived at Hotel Unique, looked around the massive lobby, no Morrissey. We got in the elevator, no sign of him. He wasn't loitering in the hallway outside our room either. We went up to the Skye Bar for dinner, and the place was so full, we were given seats at a bar that separated the restaurant from the kitchen. Half a dozen men in chef's whites were involved in the speedy, intricate business of assembling food on plates to send out to diners. It was fun to watch them. One in particular caught my eye. He had a really nice tattoo of a swallow on the side of his neck. The only people I'd ever seen with this particular tattoo were hardcore Morrissey fans, a nod to the song A Swallow on My Neck. Was this Brazilian chef a fan? I called him over during a lull and asked him.

He didn't understand what I was saying. He didn't speak English. In no time, all his other chef pals were clustered around him, listening. One of them spoke English.

"It's from a song," I said. "A Morrissey song. I was wondering if he got the tattoo because he is a Morrissey fan."

The English-speaking chef spoke to his friend in Portuguese and then said, "No. He's never heard of this song."

"Why did he get that tattoo?" I asked.

The answer came back, "Because he liked it. It's a traditional tattoo."

"Oh," I said. "Well, tell him I think it looks great."

The tattooed chef smiled shyly.

"Is he here?" the English-speaking chef asked me. "Morrissey? Is he staying here?"

"I don't know," I said. "Why? Did you hear that he was?"

"No," he shrugged. "I didn't hear anything."

After we'd finished eating, Nora and I walked out through the bar onto the rooftop pool deck where people were standing around with drinks. None of them were Morrissey.

And so, based on what the chef had said, and the fact that we weren't currently seeing him with our eyeballs, we decided that Morrissey was not staying at Hotel Unique, and the two of us relaxed.

And oh, what a place Hotel Unique was to relax in! I was so glad Nora had committed the terrible faux pas of booking it! I'd only stayed in luxury hotels a few times in my life, but when I did, the experience was never what it was cracked up to be. I hated the fawning, forelock-tugging service, the 'luxury' extras that were nothing I ever wanted or needed. The whole thing just rubbed me the wrong way.

But the staff at Hotel Unique seemed to really strike the right balance, neglecting us when it didn't matter, and really giving it their all when it was needed. Nora had left a small bag behind in the taxi from the airport, and the front desk staff had applied themselves to the task of retrieving it with all the fervor of the Scooby Gang. They didn't bother us with updates, but when we asked for them, we heard about how they'd gotten the taxi license plate from the security camera footage outside the hotel door, or were in touch with the company, trying to locate the driver.

And as for the decor of the hotel, you had to hand it to them, it really was unique. From the outside, the place really did look like a slice of watermelon. Gigantically tall doors led into the lobby decorated with whimsical wing chairs and oddly-shaped floor cushions. The guestroom hallways were moodily lit, quite dark. The elevators were frankly pitch-black, with a little red LED readout above the door that displayed the time and temperature. With the lack of air conditioning, stepping into the hot box gave the odd sensation every time of entering an oven that had just been switched on. The whole thing could have easily veered in the direction of cheesy Halloween attraction, but it was classy enough that it actually worked. I loved it there.

I especially loved our room. Our bed was a soft, downy white expanse of comfort, looking out through the big round window— one of the 'seeds' of the water-melon—onto the skyline of São Paulo. Luxury extras ranged from really awesome (a sound system you could plug into your phone that had speakers wired into the headboard of the bed) to enter-taining (a tasteful little wooden box on the nightstand containing a pack of Trident gum and two condoms.)

We stayed in bed a lot. Nora was still recovering from her bout of not-so-yellow fever, so every morning after a hearty buffet breakfast, we'd get back in bed for the after-breakfast nap.

While Nora slept, I floated on a downy cloud of comfort beside her, reading, writing in my diary or just staring out the window, thinking my thoughts.

There was a lot to think about.

Mostly, I thought about the Enneagram.

The Enneagram was a personality typing system that explained more about people's hearts, minds and motivations than any other psychological model I had ever come across in my life (and as a former self-help junkie, believe me, I had come across a fair few of them in my day). The best thing about the Enneagram was how deep it went. I had been studying it for years, had taken certification courses, taught it to clients, written books about it, and still after all this time, it constantly delivered meaningful new insights into who I was and how I related to people.

In Enneagram terms, I was a type Four, artistic, creative, sensitive and deep. Learning that I was a Four all those years ago had changed everything. It had transformed my relationship with Nora, allowed me to accept her for who she was. She was a calm and peaceful Nine, not some kind of messed-up, repressed Four who didn't like to have long conversations about her feelings. She wasn't a Four, she didn't need to express her feelings all the livelong day like I did. It wasn't a part of her personality. The Enneagram let me see that she was perfect exactly the way she was. It was a revelation.

Someone else who was perfect exactly the way he was (though he probably didn't see it that way) was Morrissey. He was a Four like me, a sensitive artist, a heart-based type who delved deep into questions of identity and selfhood. Fours were always—consciously or unconsciously—on a quest to find their true self, and often produced art along the way that was uniquely personal, and yet at the same time, spoke volumes about the universal condition of being human. This was what made Morrissey's songs so great. His voice, his aesthetic so saturated them, there was no way that anyone else could have written single line of any of those songs. And yet they spoke so truly of the universal condition of the human heart, I constantly heard fans say, "He's singing about me. That song is the story of my life."

The most beautiful thing about the Enneagram was the theory of how the nine types came to be. We all—the theory went—had all nine types within us. The pure essence qualities of the types—Goodness, Love, Value, Identity, Clarity, Awakeness, Joy, Strength, Wholeness—together made up the complete experience of being human. But as children, we couldn't hold all of that within ourselves, so we latched onto just one. We became experts on one particular aspect of being alive, and for the whole of our lives, strove to actualize it. If we were under stress, we struggled, suffering from the absence of that quality. But if we were doing well, we brought it forth in ways that inspired others, reminding them that this quality was a part of their complete self too.

As a Four, Morrissey was an expert on Identity, or rather—to give the Four essence quality its full descriptor—he specialized in Identity, Depth, Beauty, Mystery and Intimacy. He brought these qualities forth so strongly, his songs reminded us to come home to ourselves, to find that deep connection to who we really were in the core of our hearts.

He embodied these qualities so completely on stage, he was mesmerizing to watch. Here was a man simply singing a song, and yet at the same time, he was somehow expressing the beautiful unfolding mystery of what it meant to be human. It couldn't be explained, it could only be experienced, and every show was a unique window into that unfolding mystery.

Staring out the round window of our hotel room, contemplating the São Paulo skyline, I thought about the upcoming show at Teatro Renault. Unlike the massive outdoor festival conditions we'd just experienced at Primavera Fauna, this show was going to be indoors, seated, in a theater. It promised to be a much more intimate experience.

And what about Intimacy? It was one of the essence qualities associated with type Four. What did it mean? It was a word that conjured touching, closeness, sexual contact, even. But in its pure essential form, it didn't necessarily have to involve any bodies touching bodies. I knew this from my experience of Morrissey shows. He had the gift of making me feel like he was singing directly to my heart, no matter where I was in the theater. Even if I was a tiny dot up in the balcony, the true heart contact of Intimacy was in the room.

This was an interesting train of thought. In my work with the Enneagram, I had often worked to consciously connect with essence qualities. It helped with my own development, and it was a highly recommended practice when teaching clients about their type.

What if I did it here? What if I went to the show with the conscious intention of connecting to the essence quality of type Four? It was my type, it was Morrissey's type, it was something that Morrissey fans loved to connect with when they came to a show. There was sure to be oceans of it in the room. What would it be like to be consciously aware of that while experiencing it?

It felt like a really good idea. As a Four, connection, depth, intimacy, were guiding lights of my being. Having had such an amazingly tangible experience of connection with Morrissey at the show in Quito, having been at the barrier at all three shows so far, it was time for a reminder that physical proximity was not necessarily what brought Intimacy into the room. Our seats for this show were in Row F. There was no need to be greedy. If we didn't make it to the barrier this time, there was nothing to worry about. Intimacy would be in the room no matter where we ended up.

What was Intimacy like in the hour before the Morrissey show began and everyone was milling about Teatro Renault?

It was a touch scary, actually.

I'd done this before, holding essence qualities in mind, but always in extremely safe surroundings: working with a student, or at an Enneagram workshop, or sitting at home meditating. This was very very different. There was Intimacy in the room, but also hundreds and hundreds of people I didn't know, all part of a culture I didn't understand, some of them drunk, and who knew? Maybe some of them were looking for trouble.

This was definitely the case.

When we arrived, Nora and I went and greeted Alyssa, Trinity and Chayane who were standing by the barrier. The stage was a funny one. Large portions of it were slightly lower than the rest, and were labeled with signs that said 'NO STEP'. Even though the barrier was very close to the stage, there were really very few spots where Morrissey could come forward and shake hands with fans. Alyssa and Trinity were camped by one of those spots. They had clearly had a few drinks, and were in high spirits. A security guard came along and interrupted the story Alyssa was telling about their São Paulo Airbnb host who had left for Italy without leaving keys to the apartment.

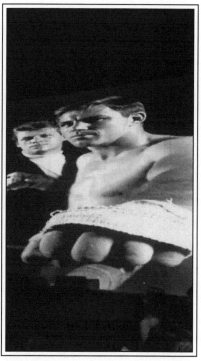

The security guard was clearly telling us to take out seats, but Alyssa played dumb.

"We don't speak Portuguese," she said. "I just don't understand what you're saying."

The guard shrugged and his supervisor stepped in, a bald, light-skinned Brazilian man the size of a small mountain, with a big attitude. He started yelling and sneering at Alyssa right from the start, and Alyssa, utterly unafraid, gave it right back to him.

It's one thing to see a high-spirited young thing like Alyssa get a bit feisty with security. It was quite another to see a grown man whose job was to keep us safe give her the finger, scream in her face, and lead the audience in derisive applause when he finally got her to walk back to her assigned seat. His behavior was so immature and inappropriate, I was frightened of what might happen if things got a little rough during the show. Someone could get hurt.

And that was indeed what happened. In the dive for the front at the end of the videos, there was what could only be described as a full-on brawl at the barrier. The bald security guard began it by lunging at Alyssa as she approached the barrier, grabbing

her hand so hard he snapped her nail off. She lost her balance
and fell so hard, her knee got horribly bloodied and banged-up.
At the same time, the guy behind Chayane took such offense at
him standing in front of him, he yanked the collar of Chayane's
t-shirt so hard, he ripped it open from neck to waist.

I'd left my seat in Row F and arrived at the barrier beside
Alyssa. Nora had been right behind me, but I'd lost her. I looked
back and she was stopped, unable to come forward because if
she did, she would block the view of a woman in a wheelchair.
Of course, someone was going to take that spot beside me on
the barrier and block the woman's view, but it couldn't be Nora.
There was absolutely no way that she could be that person.

Looking around, I vaguely saw that someone was giving a
hard time to Chayane. Not having seen how brutal he'd been, I
poked the guy and indicated the free spot on the barrier beside
me. He could leave Chayane alone and get his barrier spot. But
he looked at me, looked at the spot, shook his head politely, and
turned back to the business of pounding on Chayane.

Beside me, Alyssa was crying. I wasn't sure why. I had no idea
how badly her knee had been injured.

"I'm in so much pain," she said.

"It's okay," I said. "Morrissey's coming right now. He's going
to make everything okay."

And he did. Stunned by his arrival, everyone shaped up,
stopped hitting each other, begrudgingly made space at the barrier for the woman in the wheelchair, and the show began.

"São Paulo!" Morrissey said, before beginning Suedehead.
"November spawned a monster!"

Since the woman in the wheelchair had moved on up farther
to the right, Nora was now a couple of rows behind me, the spot
beside me on the barrier long gone. She nodded and smiled that
she was happy where she was, and looking at where I was situated, I was very happy too. In the midst of all of the chaos, I had

somehow ended up right in front of one of the narrow catwalks that came right out to the barrier. A security guard just to my left was blocking half of it with his body, so I was pretty much literally standing in the only spot where Morrissey could come out and shake hands with anyone on our whole side of the theater.

Ha. So much for Intimacy from Row F.

The handshake happened right away. During Suedehead, he came forward, reached down, and a forest of hands from behind made a grab at Morrissey's hand along with mine. A group handshake. Fun.

That was that, so it was time to get on with the business of enjoying the show. Intimacy, Depth, it felt like the Essence of Four was all around us, holding us. It was so easy to taste that feeling and try to pin it on a person. A special someone was making it happen! That person was somehow the source of all of this Mystery!

But at this show, I could see that the source was something beyond any of us, it was something holding us all. It was good to know that, to see that Morrissey wasn't holding it all up, making it happen. He was simply a catalyst, a compellingly powerful reminder that we all of us held a source of this beautiful mystery in the depth of our hearts.

It was such a delicious show. The stage was quite low and I was standing so close to it, I felt like Morrissey and the band were just inches away. The audience was massively enthusiastic right from the start, singing along in full voice for Suedehead and Alma Matters.

And then the intro to This Charming Man began. Morrissey stepped up to the microphone to sing the first line, but the whole theater was belting it out so loudly, "Punctured bicycle on a hillside desolate!" he stepped back and let us do the singing for a change. It was warm and wonderful, all held in the beautiful intimate space we were sharing.

And that space easily held connections to other shows. The opening bars of Reader Meet Author brought me back to Paris in September, the day that *List of the Lost* came out. While queueing all day, I'd read the whole book. It was an absurd, unconventionally-structured story, and I could tell that convention-bound critics would have a field day with it. But I loved it. To me, it felt like what real art should be—something that said something new, not just a slight variation on something that someone 'important' had said six months or six decades ago.

I'd brought my copy of *List of the Lost* to that show in Paris and Morrissey had paused before the encore and signed it for me. It felt like a very special moment for me, not just as a reader and a fan, but as an author. I felt really inspired by Morrissey's courage to write what was in his heart and damn the critics. His writing, the fact that he signed my copy of the book, felt like a sign. It gave me permission to follow my heart, to carry out my crazy plan of writing a deeply interior and idiosyncratic account of my South American odyssey with Morrissey. It was what my heart wanted to do, and goddammit, I was going to do it.

Morrissey, singing here in front of me in São Paulo, approached on the catwalk to the barrier. He was clearly also remembering that moment in Paris when he'd signed *List of the Lost*. As the line "reader, meet author" came out of his mouth, he took my hand and I got the most beautifully timed and wonderfully significant handshake. Reader meet author indeed! Who was who? Was each of us both?

Naturally.

And the meaning and the beauty went on, weaving itself around everything. The Elvis cover he'd been singing on this tour You'll Be Gone was perfect, delicious.

They played Mama Lay Softly on the Riverbed, a song that I knew they weren't specifically playing to honor the memory of

Nora's mother, but it felt like it. It was a song about wanting to be with your mother who has died.

"Life is nothing much to lose," Morrissey sang, "It's just so lonely here without you. So, we're going to run to you, we're going to join you, we're going to lie down beside you, mama."

Every word he sang was so filled with meaning, so touching.

At the end of the song, Gustavo and Boz, each on their respective sides of the stage joined Matt on snare drums, all three playing a military-sounding beat in unison. It was so powerful and moving, and standing as we were, right in front of Gustavo, we got to watch him play, could see his sticks hitting the drum head with complete precision. But Gustavo brought so much more than that to this short drum piece. Watching his face, it was impossible to miss the gravity and heart that he brought to the song. So beautiful.

They also played I Will See You in Far Off Places, a song that got more and more significant each time I heard it. It was fast becoming one of my favorite songs of the tour.

"Nobody knows what human life is," Morrissey sang. "Why we come, why we go. So why then do I know, I will see you, I will see you, in far off places?"

It was such a gorgeous opening to a song, diving right into the deepest question there is, the very meaning of life, and in answer, conjuring beautiful connection, and the longing for that connection all at the same time.

But just in case anyone got carried away with any highfalutin ideas about where and when connection might happen, as he sang about seeing each other in far off places, he pointed down to the stage under his feet, as if to say, Here I am! Seeing you right here! In far off São Paulo! Who'da thunk it? It's actually happening!

And it was, for sure. Connection was happening in spades. The show was like an intimate chat over the kitchen table. Morrissey even asked the audience their advice. He had been asked to appear on a local TV show called Fantastico. He asked the audience if he should do it, if it was a good idea.

"Nooo!" the audience shouted. There was a massive chorus of boos and hisses.

"So maybe one or two people are booing," Morrissey said. "Why? Because Fantastico is what?"

He walked forward on the catwalk on the other side of the stage and consulted with the fans over there.

"Because nobody on Fantastico will like me?" he said.

More shouts and boos. Apparently Fantastico was appalling.

"In that case," Morrissey concluded jokingly, "I shall go on!"

We were coming close to the end of the show when Nora, still two rows behind me, tried to tell me something. It was so loud, I couldn't hear her. Help? She wanted to help me do something? What did I need help with? She threw up her hands and gave up.

But as the show was drawing to a close with Let Me Kiss You, I suddenly got it. Nora was saying that if I intended to do a stage

invasion, she would come forward and help me.

Oh God. I had only gone over the barrier once in my life. It was at a show in Dublin about a year before, a show where Morrissey had practically killed me with song after song about the desolate condition of being alive: Smiler With Knife, Mountjoy, Asleep. It was true, it was all true, we were all trapped, dying, longing for death to come and end it. But during the last song, something in me rose up in protest. This couldn't be it. This couldn't be all there was to life. I wasn't going to lie down and take it. There had to be something more than this desolation.

Standing in that second row of the audience in Dublin, I didn't really have a lot of options when it came to "not taking it". But as a symbol of my protest, I made the only move I could, took the only route open to changing my condition. I dived at the barrier. Security pushed me back, the audience heaved me up, and I slithered over into a new place, a fresh vista, feeling great, a security guard's hand on my shoulder, marching me out into a new world. Morrissey hadn't even seen it, he'd been over on the other side of the stage, but it didn't matter. It hadn't been about him, it had been about me.

Tonight, of course, Nora was right. With this beautiful show bathed in Depth and Intimacy, there was only one correct response: to approach, to draw near, to not leave this gorgeous man alone.

In a way, Let Me Kiss You was the worst song for a stage invasion. What? Arrive at his side on the line, "You open your eyes, and you see someone you physically despise?" But then again, in this atmosphere of beauty, what song could be better to be touched during?

It didn't matter.

With all of my inner debate, the song was ending. It was too late. Morrissey was ripping off the black jacket he was wearing, tossing it into the audience, leaving the stage. The show was over. And I knew that I'd been a coward.

It hadn't been about the song. It had been about the bald security guard who was still standing two feet away from me. He'd given Alyssa and Trinity the finger a couple of times during the show, and I knew that he was itching for one of us Americans to make a move so that he'd have an excuse to give us a good pounding.

Morrissey came out for the encore, and as he sang I'm Throwing My Arms Around Paris, I felt the dawning of a second chance. Paris wasn't an appropriate stage invasion song, but yes, here it was, a rare two-song encore. The Queen Is Dead. A lively song made for a good old tumble over the barrier.

The security guard was still there, but it was time to make my protest. Did I want to walk away from this night knowing that I'd cowered in fear in front of a bully, or did I want to reach, pull myself up by my bootstraps into the gorgeous space of beauty, intimacy, depth?

Screw that security guard, I thought, here I go.

I hoisted myself up on the barrier, and he was upon me in a second, him and another security guard pushing me down by my shoulders.

I wasn't going to take it, I kept pushing forward against them.

The bald security guard was starting to use a lot of force now. Why? Where was I going to go? He opened his mouth and roared a wordless shout of threat in my face, trying to scare me down. It had about as much effect as a tiny puppy yapping at my feet. There was nothing real about this man, nothing that could hurt me.

Of course Nora didn't quite see it that way. In seconds she barged forward, her arm was around my waist, her finger jabbing the security guard in the chest.

"Don't you dare touch her! Get your fucking hands off my wife!"

Later, I wondered why I didn't stop at that point. Why didn't I make an effort to de-escalate the situation? Nora was inches away from punching this guy in the nose, and that wouldn't end well. Was I ready to bail her out of Brazilian jail?

But even though I didn't stop, Nora didn't punch him. (She told me later that a woman beside her was intoning the word "Calma, calma, calma," over and over. "I listened to her," Nora said, "and I thought to myself, she makes a good point.")

I didn't stop, but where did I think I was going with two security guards pinning me down by my shoulders? Not onto the stage. Not even over the barrier. And still, I didn't stop. I was reaching my arms towards Morrissey, up into the wide, open beautiful, gorgeous space of Intimacy. I couldn't launch my body into it, I was pinned to the ground, but nothing could stop me from reaching until the very end.

Well, there was one thing.

Morrissey approached me, took one of my flailing hands in his, and shook it for the third time that night.

"Thank you," I said, and immediately dropped down, stopping all my struggles.

("You tricked Morrissey into shaking your hand for the third time," Nora jokingly accused me later that night. "You were so much trouble, he had to come over and calma, calma, calma you down!")

But it wasn't like that at all. I hadn't been reaching for him, not specifically. I'd been reaching for what he stood for as a Four, for the space that was holding him, holding us all. I would have been happy with Intimacy from Row F. I really would. But instead I'd been given a spot at the end of the catwalk and three handshakes. And who better to give them than this beautiful man, this gorgeous Four? This ambassador of Identity, Depth, Beauty, Intimacy and Mystery?

All in all, I think the whole night turned out to be a pretty fruitful inquiry into the nature of the Essence quality of Type Four as experienced at a Morrissey show.

NOVEMBER 21, 2015
CITIBANK HALL
SÃO PAULO, BRAZIL

We spent a week in São Paulo. We had four full days off between the Teatro Renault show and the Citibank Hall show. We didn't spend literally all of that time lounging in our bed at Hotel Unique, ordering room service. We also ventured out, explored the city.

As the Boss of All Brazil, Nora decreed that one of our first outings would be to the Galeria do Rock, a shopping mall

famous for its record stores and music-themed clothes shops. We had lunch first at a fantastic restaurant, a vegan buffet called Panda Vegano where they weighed your plate and you paid by the kilo. After stuffing ourselves, we set off for the nearby Galeria do Rock on foot.

We couldn't find it, got lost. I didn't mind. I was taking in the experience of walking down this muggy Brazilian street peopled with very colorful characters. A lot of them seemed homeless or on drugs. We saw several people sleeping in bus shelters or passed out on the sidewalk.

"Wow, I've never seen that before," Nora said. "And I grew up in New York City."

"Saw what?"

"A woman just lit up her crack pipe!" Nora said. "Right out on the street!"

Had we accidentally wandered into the crack district? I didn't dare take out my phone on the street to get directions, so we stopped in a really awesome record store to look around and do some Google mapping.

We didn't go directly to the Galeria do Rock. First we stopped in another mall along the way that Nora dubbed the Galeria do Hair. It had so many wig and extension shops, tumbleweeds of fake hair had formed and were gathering in the corners of the mall. It was grungy, the escalators were ancient and rickety, and on the top floor, they didn't work at all; one was barricaded-off, steps missing like gapped teeth.

"This place is amazing," I said after we had checked out some of the stores. The first record store we'd walked into, the first thing we'd seen was Hatful of Hollow prominently displayed. The sneaker shops, the clothes shops, it was all cool stuff, things you'd actually want to buy.

"It's like what St. Mark's Place is trying to be," Nora said, "but fails because New York has sold its soul to Disney and Starbucks."

The actual Galeria do Rock was a cleaner version of this mall, with escalators that actually worked. Everything was fun to look at. Since I was in a place where I couldn't understand a single word, my visual brain was drinking in image after image, stacking up impressions.

We didn't just go to the grungy part of town. We went to the beautifully-kept Ibirapuera Park, where there were trees that looked like something out of a fairytale. We also visited the Afro Brazilian

Museum. I'd thought that there would be an audio guide available in English, but I was wrong, so we just wandered around looking, not able to understand any of the captions on the photos and displays. Taking in more impressions.

Nora recognized a face here or a name there as we walked through the museum. She was our Brazilian expert.

"The book I'm reading right now," she said, "it's about the Olympics coming to Brazil. When the author went to talk to a noted expert, some big Brazilian scholar, and told him he was writing this book, the guy said, "Brazil is not for beginners.""

That was exactly how I felt. I was looking, looking, looking, the narrative part of my brain trying to construct a story out of what I was seeing, but without understanding the language, there was nothing to go on. I saw things, things happened, and I really had no idea why. One of our Uber drivers said something to us in extremely broken English, and afterwards, I'd told Nora that I was quite sure he was telling us about a disaster, pointing out the site of a tragic fire that had occurred.

"Do you mean when he was pointing out the window, saying how bad the traffic was?"

We had no idea which one of us was right. Maybe neither.

One particularly alarming mystifying moment occurred when we were walking past a school? A courthouse? A government building? Who could say what it was, really. A crowd had gathered near the door and a handful of police were watching.

Suddenly, in the blink of an eye, the police were on top of the people (protesters?) whacking them with batons, taking them to the ground and cuffing them.

"Shit, run!" I said to Nora, and we sprinted across the street, but luckily there was no teargas, no bullets fired.

More pictures, more impressions.

A visit to the beautiful Bat- man Alley where every wall, every gate, every stoop was covered in the most wonder- ful street art. São Paulo was full of graffiti. I had seen a building ten stories tall where every single story had been tagged with the same ragged set of initials and rough hiero- glyphs. What had they done? Hired a cherry picker? Gone inside and knocked on the door of each apartment, ask- ing to lean out the window to complete the job? Seriously.

But the Batman Alley art was extremely well done. And Paris, of course, was on everyone's mind.

Our days at Hotel Unique drew to a close, and with a sigh we checked out and made our way to the not-so-unique hotel that was walking distance from Citibank Hall. Almost as soon

as we arrived, Nora presented me with a post she'd found on Facebook.

"Have you seen this?"

It was Morrissey, hanging out in the Skye Bar at Hotel Unique. Holy shit! He'd been there all along!

Aargh! Why hadn't we run into him? We could have talked! It would have been fun! But it wasn't meant to be.

It was hard not to feel a touch disappointed. But it was even harder to sustain that state of disappointment. Here we were getting ready for a show the next day. Then we were moving on to Rio, and then Brasilia, and on and on, all the way to Lima. All of it was amazing. All of it was magic. There was nothing missing. Nothing to be disappointed about.

The next morning, we arrived at Citibank Hall to spend the day queueing. I was ready for anything. To be utterly mystified, to take in beautiful impressions, perhaps for some kind of riot to break out. These were the kinds of things that happened in Brazil.

And I was not disappointed on any of these fronts.

Mystified, of course, by what everyone was saying around me. It was relaxing, in a way, to not be subjected to the invasion of having to listen to other people's tedious thoughts.

"It would be so nice if it was like this at home," Nora said. "If everyone spoke Portuguese and you never had to listen to their random blather. But with a switch so you could turn it on and off sometimes. Like in stores, it's useful, or a taxi. But really, I think you could do without it the rest of the time."

What was particularly cute was that we were in Morrisseyland, so overheard conversations sounded like this.

"Blah blah blah The Queen Is Dead blah blah blah What She Said blah blah blah Kiss Me a Lot."

Visually, I was charmed by the impressions. I couldn't resist, I went around asking people if I could take pictures of their awesome t-shirts and banners. Some spoke English, some had a nearby friend translate, others, we just mimed and smiled at each other. One young woman, Heloyse, had gotten together with her friends and made an enchanting banner that depicted Morrissey with Irish blood and a Brazilian heart.

"It's hours until the show starts," she said, holding out her hand to show us how it trembled. "And already I'm so nervous!"

There was a proper list here, the first time we'd encountered it in South America, and serious queuers who'd camped out overnight. Tension mounted, as it always did in the hour approaching

doors. Raphael, the list administrator who spoke great English, was doing a wonderful job of keeping things organized, lining people up. Trinity came by and squeezed into the spot beside me and Nora so she could borrow my phone for a minute to send a message. While she stood there, an angry chant was taken up further down the queue, more and more voices joining in.

"Fora! Fora!"

I looked at Nora.

"Are they shouting at us?"

"I don't know," she said.

Was I going to end up with my face on the pavement, a knee pressing into my back?

Raphael went by, looking harried.

"Perhaps it would be better if your friend stand outside the barrier," he said, indicating Trinity.

"She doesn't even queue," I said. "She's just using my phone."

"Yes I have explained this to them," he said. "And still it would be better."

(Later someone explained that "Fora! Fora!" meant "Out! Out!" and they were shouting it at a guy who had slipped into a spot near the front of the queue without having waited all day. The shouting made him go to the back of the line.)

What was really nice was that someone down the line took out a guitar and led a singalong. It calmed everyone down to sing along to Alma Matters. Well I know it calmed me. And I really did need calming. I felt someone's eyes on me, and turned to see the bald security guard from Teatro Renault standing by the door of the venue, arms crossed, head cocked. When he saw me looking, he held my gaze for a second, defiantly, a challenge, then turned away.

I shivered in fear. Was there going to be some kind of show-down? Retribution? For what? Attempting a stage invasion at a Morrissey show? It was ridiculous. This man just did not know how to do his job.

Doors opened and we got inside and Nora made it to the barrier before me and saved me a spot on the Boz side. Things were quiet before the videos started. I felt tired, I realized. My brain had been working overtime for days and days, trying to figure out what was happening, trying to anticipate where the next surprise would come from. It was like a cellphone searching and searching for a signal, draining the battery.

The bald security guard was there, standing in the gulf between the barrier and the stage, but a ways off, not standing right in our faces, looking for a fight. And yet, he was still being weird. He wasn't standing facing the crowd as security should. He was standing with his body angled so he could glower down the line and me and Nora and Alyssa.

Well, I hadn't come all the way to São Paulo to look at a security guard. I had come to see Morrissey. Scared, tired, it didn't matter. When he and the band walked out on stage, it all fell away. My heart, the delight of it. Here he was again. Incredible.

He walked to the front of the stage, took the microphone.

"São Paulo! São Paulo! The hour is now!" he said. "The night is yours, I am yours! Soak me in! Soak me in! Soak me in!"

His English was really quite good!

He started, as usual, with Suedehead, followed by Alma Matters, and the big Morrissey singalong was underway.

There was a lot that was really quite adorable about the way that South American fans sang along at concerts. First was the fact that they sang along at all. These songs were in English. It really surprised me that South American fans sang along just as much, if not more, than fans in England and the States. And they did so in adorably accented English—often the most heavily accented singers belting out the lyrics with greatest gusto. It was really entertaining.

But I think the thing that tickled me the most about how South American fans sang along was that they didn't just sing along to the words. When it came to songs like Suedehead and First of the Gang, they also sang along to the intro that Jesse played on the guitar. In South America, Suedehead did not begin with 'Why do you come here?' it began with a chorus of 'Do do do do do do do, Do do do do do do do' from the audience.

And Morrissey! What tickled and surprised me about him

 in South America was how much he talked to the audience. I had naively assumed that he would speak hardly at all between songs because these weren't English-speaking countries. But of course these were his fans, and lots of them spoke excellent English. In fact, a lot of the fans I had spoken to had been inspired to learn English because of Morrissey, because they wanted to understand him better.

So when he chatted away in English, he was understood. Mostly.

He brought up the topic of the awesome graffiti that was all over São Paulo. I gave a loud whoop of agreement. It was one of the most strikingly awesome things about the city.

"I wonder when they do it," he said.

"Now!" I shouted.

"Now?" he said. "Hmmm!"

I could just see it, a graffiti artist working under the cover of night. All eyes in the city turned towards Morrissey, everyone's attention glued to him. The artist could probably sneak into this very theater and paint a mural on the back wall, cherry picker and all, and we wouldn't even notice. Our attention was so riveted to the stage.

It wasn't an image that lent itself to the snappy repartee of a heckle, so I wasn't able to get it across.

After the show, I was approached by a fan who spoke very good English.

"I have a question," he said. "Why did you shout "No!" at Morrissey?"

I had no memory of shouting "No!" at Morrissey, so this question really confused me. But eventually it became clear that he was talking about my "Now!" heckle. (Não in Portuguese means No.) The mystification apparently went both ways.

Morrissey talked a lot that night. He talked about how much he sweated ("My head gets wet. My brain gets wet.") He talked about religion ("There are eight different Gods in the world, and none of them make an appearance to intervene. And so, I give up.")

Unfortunately, he had to stop and talk in the middle of a song.

Jesse started a quiet intro on the guitar and I leaned back delighted into Nora's arms, settling down to hear the beautiful and dark meditation on death Smiler With Knife. I don't know who Morrissey's smiler is, but when I hear that song, the serial killers who spring to my mind are cancer doctors.

The rest of the audience were not settling down quietly to listen, though. There were too many whoops and hollers as Morrissey sang the first few lines.

He broke off, and Jesse stopped playing.

"Shall I stop?" he asked us. "Do you need to make a phone call? Have you lost your hat?"

Oh no, this song was too good to abandon because of a few oafish loudmouths.

"Sing!" I pleaded. "Sing!"

"Should I sing?" he said.

"Please," I begged. "Oh please!"

"Sim!" the audience answered.

"We'll be good!" Nora promised.

And he proceeded with the rest of the song. It was glorious, beyond amazing.

A feature of South American shows that I really enjoyed was how the band was introduced. Instead of Morrissey doing his usual, "From Austin, Texas, Gustavo Manzur, from Austin, Texas, Jesse Tobias...etc." each member of the band was walking up to the microphone in turn and introducing themselves. It was very fun to hear them speak. There was a little bit of English, a little bit of Spanish, and a little bit of Portuguese.

I also enjoyed how Morrissey accepted flags and banners from fans (I was especial-ly happy for Heloyse when he took her Irish Blood, Brazilian Heart banner) and took the time to auto-graph books and albums.

One fan had really gone all-out on this front. He was holding the album Ringleader of the Tormen-tors up to be autographed, and he had dressed up in a tuxedo that matched what Morrissey was wearing on the album cover. He offered the album up to Morrissey all throughout the show, and Morrissey eventually took it, but, oh, bad luck! The marker he handed with it failed to work. Morrissey shrugged and handed the album back unsigned.

Nora had a Sharpie, and we tried to rescue the situation by giving it to the fan, seeing if he'd get a second go. I was really rooting for him. He had inadvertently been such an enormous help throughout the show. Holding up the album so diligently, he had blocked my view of the bald security guard with it pretty much every time I looked in that direction. It was as if he wasn't there at all.

But it was too late for this fan, Morrissey never came back to him, he'd missed his only shot.

Morrissey's last song before he left the stage was What She Said. It was, as always, a rip-roaring good song. He whipped the microphone cord around with a lot of flair during it, but something went funny in the end. He went to exit the stage, and found that the microphone cord had gotten tangled in the ornaments he had dangling from his belt loops. One of the crew had to go down on his knees and untangle the cord, like a parent patiently untangling a child's hopeless knot. When it was undone and he was freed, he came back and gave a little wave to the audience, as if to say, Sorry about that, now the show is actually over, off I go! My heart melted.

For the encore, he again did I'm Throwing My Arms Around Paris, followed by The Queen Is Dead. He took a flag during the latter and tucked it into his belt.

"He's like a Brazilian merman!" Nora said when we saw Alyssa's picture of it later on Facebook.

At Hotel Unique, there had been a pool in the basement where there were underwater speakers, so you could actually hear music while you swam. I wasn't much of a swimmer, hated to put my head underwater, but Nora was a real water baby, this pool was made for her.

When she came back from her swim, she'd talked about what would be the best thing ever.

"A Morrissey concert underwater!" she said. "It would be so great!"

Starring this Brazilian merman, of course.

And really, that was what it would take to top these shows that we were seeing. It was pure magic, all of it. And we weren't even halfway done.

RIO DE JANEIRO, BRASILIA & SALVADOR

Our remaining time in Brazil flew by. Everything was beautiful, fascinating, each show we saw more amazing than the last. There were memories to treasure, unforgettable moments that left indelible impressions.

One of those moments happened at the show in Rio de Janeiro. It was an extraordinary night. The audience was like nothing I had ever seen. Standing as I was at the barrier, I had the whole massive crowd at my back, and every single person in that whole venue was singing along to every word. It was incredible. The audience felt like it had one huge voice. The thousands and thousands of people began swaying in unison in time to the music. We became one entity, a thousand-armed body, reaching forward to Morrissey. We were a creature with a thousand-chambered heart, spilling forth the joyful ecstasy of seeing him at last.

It all went off-the-charts when This Charming Man began. I just remember trying—and failing—to sing. It was so fun, it was so amazing, I remember opening my mouth, attempting to sing along. But every time, all that came out of me was helpless laughter. I was incapacitated by joy, swimming in a sea of the sweetest Moz love.

I think it was the best two minutes and thirty seconds of my life.

And Rio itself? Well, it was the most fetching city I have ever had the pleasure of laying eyes on. The beaches, the gorgeous hills, every fresh vista was utterly enchanting. And of course—of course—in this magical place, all my dreams came true.

I saw el mono.

Just as promised, on a path leading up to a hill called Sugar-loaf, there he was. Him and his seven cousins, jumping around in the trees, scampering down onto the railing, curiously check-ing us out, posing for pictures.

These were unusual monkeys, marmosets. They didn't have the prehensile tails, or the classic-friendly-monkey look. Staring into their wizened human-looking faces, the intelligence in their eyes was electric. It made me think of a Harry Potter spell gone wrong, a person turned into a shrunken, furry beast.

And just in case we felt we were missing out, the next day we saw the more classic fun-loving, swinging-in-the-tree kind of monkeys in Parque Lage. At least a dozen of them moving around up in the branches. We got to stand for a long time, watch one tear apart a giant fruit and eat it, ripping off bites, looking down at us every few seconds to see if we were still there.

The transition from Rio's beauty to Brasilia's, um, architec-ture felt like some kind of practical joke.

Really? A city made of soulless concrete blocks was someone's idea of a good idea?

But it didn't take anything away from our short visit there. The venue—made of soulless blocks of corrugated iron (old shipping containers)—was wonderful. The day we spent waiting outside it was one of the nicest Morrissey queues ever. Brasilia was Morrissey's last stop in Brazil, and we got to spend time for the last time with the utterly adorable Brazilian fans who had taken us into their hearts. We were all Mozfriends now, it was a truly special bond.

And there was music! Guitarist Ian and singer Ricardo led a singalong, knew all the words, even took requests. We sang and sang, ending, of course, with South America's favorite singalong song, Alma Matters.

Later that night, during the show, it was time for Alma Matters again. I was singing along with all of my Brazilian friends, when Morrissey appeared suddenly in front of me at the edge of the stage. He was there for a handshake! As I took his hand, I couldn't help wondering, What's this for? A handshake initiated by Morrissey is so special, I couldn't help seeing it as some kind of reward. For singing Alma Matters so beautifully? For perfect attendance at the barrier so far in South America?

It was silly to try to guess, so I let it go. It wasn't a

night to hold onto things. The show was clear, beautiful, unencumbered. Light. Morrissey was so clearly and beautifully being himself, everything he sang ringing so true in the heart.

The moment that stuck with me though, was during You Have Killed Me. For some reason, Morrissey had hauled the microphone stand over to our side of the stage, and was singing it right in front of us.

"Piazza Cavour, what the hell is my life for?" he implored, then added a barked and bitter, "Nothing! Nothing!"

It was, of course, freshly minted, from the core of his heart, 100% authentically what he felt.

And I just did not agree. How could he stand there and say that?

"Singing!" I contradicted, shouting up at him. "Your life is for singing!"

How could he not know? Really! Did he need to be told? It was so obvious. He had been put on this planet to do exactly what he was doing right at that moment. He was doing it so perfectly. He had done it perfectly all the way from Quito and, fingers crossed, would keep doing it all the way to Lima. The most gifted artist, the composer and transmitter of the purest messages of the heart, the representative for all of us of the 'I' that was at the core of our humanity? Standing up there and saying that he didn't know what his life was for?

Seriously!

And so we said goodbye to Brasilia, but still had one more stop in Brazil, a side trip to Salvador on the northeast coast. We stayed in Pelourinho, the historical district, in a hotel on a narrow, cobbled pedestrian street. When we checked in, the clerk told us about the musical experiences we could enjoy during our visit. He warned us that a lot of music in Salvador was percussion based, "more bumping than other kinds of music." Nora and I were both drum students, so we spent a very happy few days in Salvador, following drum troupes as they danced down the street, taking in shows where people played the most excellent kind of bumping music.

We didn't forget Morrissey entirely while in Salvador, though. We spent a day with local fan Renata, who took us on a whirlwind tour of the rest of the city and gave us the local's point-of-view. Renata was sick to death of the traditional Brazilian music that Nora and I found so enchanting, and bemoaned the lack of a real indie rock scene. Of course we also talked a lot about Morrissey and how much he meant to us.

Renata told us that she and her husband had tried for a long, long time to have a baby. Finally they had given up and instead of continuing with the expensive fertility treatments, they'd spent the money on traveling to England to see some Morrissey shows. It had an amazing experience, and against all odds, during the trip Renata finally became pregnant with her son. "Someone once joked to me that it was Morrissey's baby," Renata told us with a smile.

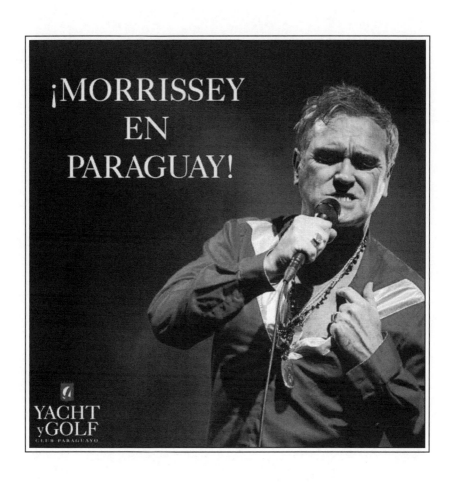

DECEMBER 6, 2015
YACHT Y GOLF CLUB
ASUNCIÓN, PARAGUAY

We flew from Salvador in Brazil to Asunción in Paraguay. Like all of the flights on the tour so far, it was on time, smooth, no problems. Except I noticed that there were lots of tiny irritants during the flight. The guy beside me elbowed me incessantly, there was a crying baby who just wouldn't settle, a woman behind me with a hacking cough. So many things, and it kept coming. A massive, slow line at immigration. A woman behind us in the line for customs who insisted on bumping up against Nora's legs with her suitcase every single time we moved forward in line. I gallantly let Nora walk ahead of me and took her spot. None of this affected me. Nothing could get me down, not the crying baby, not the coughing, not even getting bumped in the legs with a suitcase 20 times in a row. Because we were on our way to the most amazing place in Paraguay. No! The most amazing place in all of South America.

The Yacht y Golf Club.

I knew it made no sense. It was utterly nuts. Asunción was a provincial city, a backwater. What could possibly be so amazing about the Yacht y Golf Club?

But I'd had an intuition about this place when I'd booked it, and my heart would not be argued with. Something super special was going to happen here.

It was a feeling, just a feeling. But a feeling that I couldn't help trying to explain to myself.

Maybe, I told myself as we got into the cab, it's because we've made it here. Simply getting this far in the tour is such an achievement. Me, Nora and Morrissey, all healthy enough to turn up for all of these shows? A massive achievement. Or maybe it's because the Yacht y Golf Club is the venue for the show, plus the hotel we get to stay at? That has never happened before. That could be super special. If everyone is staying here? Maybe we'll all get to hang out in the bar: us fans, the crew, the band. And who knows? Even Morrissey might make an appearance. How special would that be?

We got in a cab and took in our first impressions of Asunción. It seemed incredibly poor, even by South American standards. We drove past emaciated animals standing by the side of the road, kids stuffed precariously on the backs of motorbikes, and dusty barefoot children selling food to drivers stopped at the light.

I took out my phone and texted Alyssa to see if she'd arrived already. She had.

"Bad news tho," she typed. "The gig is 99% canceled."

My heart sank so low, I don't think it was even in the taxi anymore, it felt like it was being dragged along the rough potholed street under the cab.

Why?

"The venue flooded."

Asunción, apparently, in the days before we had arrived, had
suffered from a catastrophic storm. The whole city had been
flooded. There was massive property damage, electricity was still
out in parts of the city, phones weren't working properly, and
the venue, an outdoor stage at the Yacht y Golf Club set up right
on the bank of the Paraguay river, was under a couple of feet of
water.

"I don't know if they'll reschedule or just cancel," Alyssa
typed. "We'll see."

This was dreadful. What kind of special was this turning out
to be?

We arrived at the Yacht y Golf Club, which luckily had
electricity and started the check-in process. If there wasn't going
to be a gig, why were we even here? Could there still be something special that would happen this weekend? Morrissey and
the band and crew were staying here right?

Wrong.

We ran into some fans who told us that Morrissey and everyone else had originally been set to stay here, but they'd all moved
to a hotel in another part of town.
Why? Nobody knew.

When the guy at the front desk
heard us talking about Morrissey,
he said, "You know the concert is
not tomorrow night?"

"Yes," we said.

"Maybe Sunday, yes?" he said.

"Hopefully," I said.

Maybe this was all just a blip.
Maybe the show would go on, just
a day late. We'd change our flights,
get a room here for an extra night, and everything would go
ahead as planned.

"If it's on Sunday," I asked the man at the desk, "would you have a room free so we could stay an extra night?"

He checked the computer.

"No," he said, "we are fully booked."

It was a dismal evening. There was no box office at the Yacht y Golf Club, so we took a taxi downtown to the Hotel Guarani and circumnavigated the building before we found the tiny ticket booth sandwiched between it and the Hard Rock Café. We picked up our tickets that now said that the show would be on Sunday instead of Saturday. But was this really guaranteed? What if there was more rain? The forecast wasn't great. We changed our flights anyway, and hoped for the best.

We met up with Alyssa and European fan Elina who had joined the tour in Brazil, and with two French fans Aubry and Nico who had come all the way from Europe for this one show. We sat and had drinks at the hotel, a very glum gathering. Alyssa's airline was penalizing her enormously for changing her flight, she was losing hundreds and hundreds of dollars, and Aubry and Nico weren't even sure if they would get to see Morrissey at all having come all this way.

I went to bed that night feeling so heavy, like my chest was lined with lead and dreamed that I was going to a Morrissey show where the ticket was a raspberry, held in a room that I couldn't find because I'd practiced leaving the room over and over, but I'd never practiced arriving in it.

The dream was perfect, a reminder. In fact, everything that had happened since our arrival in Asunción had been a big wake-up call, I'd just been too miserable to pay attention to it. I got out of bed the next morning and resolved to get a hold of myself, to do what the dream was telling me to do, to practice arriving.

As an Enneagram type Four, I was massively prone to getting lost in thoughts, feelings, daydreams, fantasies. I could get so lost in a flight of fancy, all awareness of 'real' reality would drop away, and I would have no sense at all of what was happening in my surroundings, or that I even had a body.

Meditation and awareness work were absolutely vital for me because of this. I needed to get grounded. I needed to constantly be reminded that I had a body. I needed to practice arriving in the present moment over and over again. Learning to meditate had been a godsend, planting my ass on a cushion and gluing my awareness to each breath, no matter what amazingly fascinating thoughts and daydreams came to try to tempt me away. But it didn't stop there. I'd also learned ways to ground myself, by paying continuous attention, say, to the soles of my feet as I walked, or the taste of food as I ate. Being aware of how my senses connected me to the world around me was a massively effective way to genuinely arrive in the present moment, and I could see that I needed some help in arriving properly here at the Yacht y Golf Club. I got to work right away.

Breakfast was bedlam. There was some kind of soccer tournament happening in town and swarms of teen soccer teams jammed the breakfast buffet. Nora found us a table, cleared off the dirty dishes, and as we ate, I didn't retreat inside myself, adding the loud teens to the ever-evolving sad story of the Yacht y Golf Club Flood Disaster. Instead, I stayed with the taste of my food, the experience of sound entering my ears, the quality of taking things in through my vision.

It started clearing things up right away.

I woke up from the story I thought I was living.

What was this heaviness and sadness all about? I felt robbed. Why? Because I hadn't been given the fairytale weekend at the Yacht y Golf Club that I felt I deserved. A fairytale I'd dreamed up based on an intuition that something special would happen here?

Well I was so mired in this made-up story and how it wasn't panning out, it was quite possible that I would completely miss

the something special, even if it happened right under my nose. The breakfast room had plate-glass windows that faced the Paraguay River. Clumps of floating vines, some as big as tiny islands, drifted slowly by on the surface of the water, carried along by the current of the river. I'd never seen anything like them.

"Let's go outside after breakfast," I said to Nora. "I want to see what this place is like."

The grounds of the Yacht y Golf Club were huge, sprawling. There were tons of tennis courts, a golf course, and a long riverfront where all the boats were docked. There was also a beach.

The venue, which was right beside one of the swimming pools, was looking good. No signs of flooding, and people were busy at work, setting it up. The sky was cloudy, but there was no sign of rain.

Even the newspaper seemed sure that the show was going to happen tomorrow night.

So here we were with an unexpected free day on our hands. The weather was warm and muggy. The Yacht y Golf Club's multiple swimming pools called out to Nora. But I didn't want to spend my day splashing around in the pool.

El concierto de Morrisey se realiza mañana, en el Yacht

Preparativos. Últimos detalles en el escenario del show.

Primera vez. Morrissey, ex vocalista de The Smiths, debuta en un escenario paraguayo mañana, a las 21.00.

El show del cantante británico Morrisey, que debía realizarse esta noche, se pospone para mañana, a las 21.00. Será el primer concierto en Paraguay del ex líder del grupo The Smiths, en el Court Central del Yacht y Golf Club Paraguayo. Las entradas siguen en venta en Ticketea, desde G. 260.000.

Los portones abrirán a las 18.00, mientras que desde las 20.00 el público podrá ver un material audiovisual que es

ofrecido por el equipo de Morrisey. Según la productora del show, CSPro, el video intacta sobre el estilo de vida que lleva el artista, comprometido en contra de la monarquía, a favor de los derechos humanos, exacerbado vegetariano y defensor de los animales.

DETALLES. Steven Patrick Morrisey, de 55 años, llega a suelo paraguayo como parte de una gira regional que incluye países como Ecuador, Chile, Brasil, Argentina, Uruguay y Perú.

A saber:
Evento: Concierto de Morrisey.
Lugar: Court Central del Yacht y Golf Club Paraguayo.
Fecha: Mañana, desde las 21.00. Los portones de lugar se abrirán a las 18.00 y a las 20.00 se proyectará un material audiovisual.

Su álbum más reciente es *World peace is none of your business* (2014) y en su show no faltarán canciones como *Suedehead, Now my heart's full, like sunday, y First of the gang to die.* Además, se anuncian títulos como *The more you ignore me, the closer I get, y About* *matter.*

Como el británico es ve-

getariano, solicitó a la producción que no se venda comida a base de carne a su alrededor por lo que se evitará el expendio en las cercanías del Court central.

Además, pidió verduras y frutas orgánicas, leche de almendras, agua de manantial Fiji, vino Chianti y exige que la comida que consumirá se cocine frente a él.

Entradas: Campo, G. 260.000; Preferencia, G. 365.000; y Campo Vip, G. 700.000. Los boletos están disponibles en la red Ticketea.
Informes: 415-7500

There was something important I needed to do. Something I'd been putting off. Going on an extended tour like this, there was an illusion that there was all the time in the world, endless shows lined up, stretching all the way to Lima. But the shock of the flood and the show maybe being canceled woke me up to reality. And the reality was that we were totally delusional if we thought we had any control over anything. At any moment there could be a flood, a fire, an accident. A microscopic infection could take the whole tour down right now. The grand plans we all had were just a huge fantasy. The only thing that could be banked on was what was happening right here in the present. It was the only thing that was in any way real.

I'd certainly cooked up my own grand plans around this tour. My intention was to have the trip of a lifetime, and then go home and write a book about the whole adventure. It would be a magnificent book. There would be lavish descriptions of the best Morrissey shows ever. Plus amazing photographs. And monkeys. And a really funny scene with a thermometer in a sex toy shop. It would be such a great book. Everything I would ever need to say about music, Morrissey and monkeys would be captured in its pages forever. If Morrissey ever wanted to know what I thought about him or his South American tour, he could read my book and know it all.

Ha! Yes, there was this theoretical book in the theoretical future that Morrissey might theoretically read. But right now at the Yacht y Golf Club, that was still all a fantasy.

What about now? After seven of the most beautiful shows ever, was there really nothing to say to him right here in the present? I was going to be standing right in front of him tomorrow night. Did I really have nothing to offer in response to his outpouring of beauty? Just an idea that I would one day write a book?

I parked myself under an umbrella on the pool deck, took out my notebook, and wrote a letter to Morrissey. It wasn't very long. Okay, yes, seven pages could be considered long under some circumstances, but I had a book's worth of words about Morrissey and South America bubbling around inside me, so seven pages was really quite restrained.

This letter was about being in the present, so as I folded it up and sealed the envelope, I made a promise to myself. Delivering this letter wasn't going to become some big thing, a drama or distraction from being present at the show. I was going to offer it to him here at the show at Yacht y Golf Club, and if he couldn't take it because the barrier was too far from the stage, I would offer it to him one more time at the theater show in Buenos Aires where we had front row seats. If he didn't take it then, I would happily throw it in the bin, accepting that writing it was a valuable lesson in being in the present, but the letter itself wasn't actually something Morrissey needed to read.

The next day was the show day. We got up and got on line at 8am. We were the first to arrive, and were soon joined by Alyssa, and Brazilian fan Vanessa. The weather was perfect, warm and sunny. We set up camp on the patio of the snack bar and had a quiet and luxurious morning, lounging around, ordering drinks and snacks, watching workmen busily setting up barriers and booths and tents.

After lunch, we discovered that throughout the morning, security had directed arriving fans to form a line outside the fence of the property, so we gathered up our things and went and joined the rest of the queue, where we were warmly welcomed into the front of the line.

This was Morrissey's first time playing in Paraguay, and the Paraguayan fans we met were really quite amazed and excited that Morrissey had come all the way to Asunción to see them.

I think the most excited fan of all was Gustavo. His banner had a quote from Morrissey's Autobiography:

It was a really nice afternoon on line. I really like spending time around people who like to sing, and Gustavo was one of those people. He was so happy about the show, he would every now and then spontaneously burst into song, just one line. "I would go out tonight, but I haven't got a stitch to wear!" or "Bigmouth, la da da da da!"

And when it came to sound check time, well! Sound check at an outdoor venue like this was very special. There were no walls to muffle the sound, so everyone on line could hear everything crystal clear, from the crewmember checking the microphones, "Check, hey, two, check, hey," all the way through to the whole band testing the system by running through whole songs from start to finish (minus the vocals, of course).

It was really a wonderful setup, the perfect opportunity for Morrissey karaoke. Everyone knew the words, and we were singing along to—well we were singing along to the real thing. The band started with Suedehead and with me and Gustavo leading the pack, we had a good singalong going in no time. It was really fun.

We sang and sang and before we knew it, we were getting closer to doors. The line was divided into two rows of men, two rows of women. The sun set behind the bamboo fence. And even though I tried to optimize things by having the security guard pre-search my bag as I stood waiting in front of her, when the signal was given and we dashed for the entrance, my ticket taker took so long to scan my ticket, people were streaming past me. Luckily one of those people was Nora, so our spot on the barrier was never in jeopardy. We ended up on the Boz side, and sat for a while before the show began to watch the sky get dark and the place fill up.

It was an absolutely beautiful night. The sky deepened into an almost metallic blue, with wispy clouds turning the pink of cotton candy. Off to our right, a single star hung low on the horizon. It must have been a planet, it was so bright. I remembered, for the hundredth time that day, to be present, to occupy my body by connecting to my senses. My ear tuned into the sounds around me, the clop-clop of people walking up the metal stairs to the bar, the happy hum of conversation rising from the crowd.

I did my usual loving kindness practice towards Morrissey, the band, the crew. I moved on to fans, happily including Nico and Aubry, who'd made it to the show after all, and fretting for a moment when I got to Chayane, who nobody'd seen all day. He was on a long-haul bus trip from São Paulo that had clearly gotten delayed. But as soon as I pictured him in my mind's eye and wished him well and safe, he magically appeared before me, giving me a little wave from his spot a few rows back.

The sky grew dark, the pre-show videos came and went, and finally the moment came where Morrissey and the band took the stage. The excitement of the crowd was huge.

Before he started singing, Morrissey took the microphone and proclaimed, "On this day of days, peace and justice, republic or death!" and the first chord of Suedehead rang out on the guitar.

Even before Morrissey sang the first line of the song, everyone was singing, a loud chorus of "do do do do do do do" accompanying Jesse's opening riff on the guitar.

"Why do you come here?" Morrissey sang.

The answering cheers and screams and whoops from the audience said it all. The people of Paraguay came because they utterly adored Morrissey. The whole place was singing along, delight and excitement in every word.

"Why do you telephone?" Morrissey sang, "And why do you send me silly notes?"

In my hand, I waved the little seven-page note that I had written. The stage was very far away, and really high up. There was no way that he could reach down and take it, so I put it away until the next show in Buenos Aires.

Alma Matters was next, and it was clear that Morrissey was feeling a warm and lovely connection with the audience. Alma Matters was a song during which Morrissey often shook hands with fans at the barrier. Even though he was so far from us, there was no way he could possibly reach, he still offered his hand to people in the front row during the line, "Because to someone, somewhere, oh yes, Alma matters..." As he did, someone at the front row tossed a Paraguayan flag up to him and he caught it and waved it around to the massive delight and approval of the audience.

The enthusiasm of the crowd was just wonderful. The sweet-ness with which they cheered for Morrissey, the love that was pouring out of them was so palpable. When First of the Gang began, there was a massive cheer, delighted screams, and again everyone sang along with Jesse's intro on the guitar. First of the Gang is an utterly singable song, and right from the start, people were jumping, clapping, singing along to every word, whether they could sing in tune or pronounce the words in English or not. The song is one of those Morrissey masterpieces, full of paradoxical emotion, the good and the bad, side by side, neither canceling the other out. It is, in short, the happiest song about a dead member of a street gang you are ever likely to hear.

When Morrissey got to the chorus, "Hector was the first of the gang with a gun in his hand, the first to do time, the first of the gang to die!" the whole place was belting it out along with him in joyful full voice.

By the time we got to the
closing lines about Hector,
that lovable rogue who "stole
all hearts away," it was clear
that Morrissey had stolen
Paraguay's heart away, and
there was no doubt as he put
his hand on his heart that he
was feeling the love too.

Morrissey wasn't only one
affected by the enormous
warmth and affection that
was pouring out of the audience. The band seemed to
be feeling it too. A couple of
time, I caught Boz looking
out at the crowd, an incredu-
lous look on his face like, Is
this really happening?

Because the stage was so high, and we were so close to it, I
could only see Jesse when he walked up to the front for his solos, but that didn't mean that I wasn't noticing him. There was
something extraordinary about the way he was playing. His solos during World Peace Is None of Your Business were massive,
like the love of the crowd had supercharged his performance.
It really hit me again during Kiss Me a Lot, and so many other
times throughout the show. I really wished I was closer to him
so I could see what he was up to. I promised myself that if I got
the chance, I would take in the next few shows on his side of the
stage to get the full-frontal blast of his guitar magic.

The show was perfect, the night was alive. How could I have
ever doubted my heart's intuition that something truly special
would happen here at Yacht y Golf Club?

The show moved on, and Morrissey delivered song after song that spoke to that paradox of light-and-dark, joy-and-sorrow. Sometimes it was the audience that held one side, and him the other, like when he sang How Soon Is Now? This is one of the most unremittingly dark songs Morrissey has ever written, and unlike some of the songs he co-wrote with Johnny Marr, the darkness is not alleviated by an up-tempo beat or cheerful guitar riffs.

"There's a club if you'd like to go," Morrissey sang, walking over to the side of the stage, approaching the audience. "You could meet somebody who really loves you." He sang, of course, as he always did, like this was freshly occurring to him. "So you go and you stand on your own, you leave on your own, you go home and you cry and you want to die!" He cut off the last word with a sudden whip of the microphone cord, turning away from the audience, as if he could not bear to reveal the shame of this memory while looking at another human being.

How Soon Is Now? is one of the most painful songs ever, but at the same time, it is the most well-loved piece of anything that Morrissey has ever written. And so the crowd in Asunción went wild, loving every second of howling those heart-scalding lyrics along with Morrissey, "I am human and I need to be loved!" What could be more fun than that? Nothing, if the reaction of the crowd in Asunción was anything to go by.

When paradox appears, it's so tempting to try to simplify it, to collapse an experience into one side or other. Standing there watching Morrissey, I felt so grateful to him for existing. His music, and especially his presence on stage, invited an opening to paradox, allowing the heart to have a full experience that didn't always come down to choosing sides. My weekend at the Yacht y Golf Club was perfect, not because everything had gone well, or according to plan—clearly a flooded venue and a postponed show was not anyone's idea of things going well—but because I could be there fully, letting my heart communicate with him in the words of gratitude I had written in my letter, letting my heart be here now to experience this amazing night.

Gratitude for all of it overflowed in my heart. For the good things, yes, but also for the space Morrissey held open for the bad things—the loneliness, the shame—all the unacceptable aspects of ourselves were held in the music too. Nothing was left out. All of us could be present.

And then a hush fell as Gustavo started his solo piece on the piano. Gustavo always played this piece so beautifully, but tonight, you could hear that he was bringing something extra to it. His heart too, it seemed, was reaching out to Paraguay through the music, responding in kind to the outpouring of audience love. The piece reached its crescendo and morphed into the opening strains of Everyday Is Like Sunday.

Oh! The audience gave a heartfelt shout of recognition and approval that echoed everything I was feeling.

"Trudging slowly over wet sand," Morrissey sang, "back to the bench where your clothes were stolen."

It was a desolate opening to a song, for sure, and things really don't get better.

"This is the coastal town that they forgot to close down. Armageddon! Come Armageddon! Come Armageddon, come!"

And yet at the same time, running alongside this lonely desolation, there was this melody, this music that sounded like a resurrection, like sun breaking through clouds, like a heart filled up with hope.

This hope was present with the despair, not canceling it out. Both were there, intertwined in every line that Morrissey sang, every gesture and movement, every breath he took. He was living the message of this song, he was hope and despair. Standing there on stage, he was a beautiful symbol of that paradox—the heart that can open up to everything that is here, even if it seems to contradict itself.

And that wasn't all! He was humor too.

"Trudging back over pebbles and sand," he sang. "And a strange dust lands on your hands, and on your face."

Here, bright lights came up, shining out directly onto the audience. Morrissey came to the front of the stage, looking out at us. He pointed at us, gesturing at our faces. As he did, someone threw a flower that hit him right in the face, but he didn't flinch, he playfully tried to catch it, but it fell out of his grasp. More flowers immediately followed, and he caught one deftly and flicked it cheekily into the crowd on the words, "On your face!"

The lights went down again and the song drew to a close that felt like it was epic. Inside my heart, up on stage, in the audience, there was a massive Yes to the space of the heart where we could be present with it all—hope, loneliness, longing, despair, anything that we had to bring. Everyone could share grease tea together, nothing left out.

Let Me Kiss You came soon after that, and on the line, "You open your eyes, and you see someone you physically despise," Morrissey ripped off his white shirt, mopped his brow with it and tossed it into the audience to tumultuous cheers and screams. As the song ended, Boz and Jesse came and stood at the edge of the stage directly in front of us, Boz, as always, vigilantly keeping an eye on the shirt melee as it was torn apart by fans.

We were getting to the point in the show where I was afraid the show was ending because Morrissey had left the stage, but he reappeared wearing a blue shirt. He took the microphone to introduce the next song.

"Of course, as we all know, most people on the planet, they don't actually have any taste. But the worst thing is, they don't actually care. In fact—"

Here he was interrupted by heckles from the audience. I couldn't understand what they were shouting.

"I don't know," he answered in a funny accent. "I really don't know."

It was hard to tell if he was answering an actual question, or just pretending.

Then he continued. "You could almost say—if you had the time—that the world is full of crashing bores."

The song was beautiful, they all were. I didn't want the show to end, but when he began The Queen Is Dead, I knew that it was over. He left the stage after the song, came back quickly for the encore. Before he launched into the very final song of the night,

he gave us a few words of advice.

"Just remember," he said, "be true to yourself, hold onto your friends, be good to your mother, be kind to animals, and if you have a god, she or he will watch over you. I love you."

Then he sang This Charming Man, and when he came to the line, "I would go out tonight, but I haven't got a stitch to wear," he ripped his shirt open halfway, revealing his chest, much to the delight of the audience. The second time he sang the line, he ripped it the rest of the way open and took it off entirely, wiped the sweat off his brow with it, and played with it while he sang, until he finally tossed it into the audience and left the stage for good.

DECEMBER 9 & 10, 2015
TEATRO OPERA ALLIANZ & LUNA PARK
BUENOS AIRES, ARGENTINA

I liked Buenos Aires as soon as I laid eyes on it. It was a really charming city, full of wide boulevards, historic buildings, and pretty public gardens. It made me think of Paris with the sidewalk cafés, theaters. There was even an obelisk. Not an authentic Egyptian one, this one was made quite a bit more recently, but it still made me smile.

The obelisk was at the end of the street our hotel was on. At the other end of the street was Luna Park, the big indoor venue where the second Buenos Aires Morrissey show would take place. And in the middle of the street was Teatro Opera, the seated venue for the first show.

Being so close to everything made me feel like I was staying in a Parisian-inspired Morrissey theme park. Arriving during a big holiday weekend, the Feast of the Immaculate Conception, added to the effect. The streets were deserted. I went out into the warm sunny afternoon looking for some local currency, and the by-now-legendary OCA where I was supposed to pick up our tickets for the Luna Park show.

The OCA did turn out to be something like a FedEx office, and like most other businesses, was closed and would be for days because of the holiday. But luckily, when I swung past Luna Park, I saw that the box office was open, and without any fuss at all, picked up our tickets there. Why couldn't they just have told me to do that in the email? Why such terrifying byzantine instructions that had made me fret for months?

And currency? The only other people out on the street were shady characters loitering on corners murmuring "cambio, cambio, cambio" as I walked by. In my research I had made a note about forgery being big business in Buenos Aires. "Watch out, taxi drivers will try to pass you bad bills!" Even though everyone bought their currency on the street because the exchange rate was so much better, I could not bring myself to take out my wallet and hand money to one of these people. I took the hit and went to the ATM.

We made our way out to dinner that evening, walking through the quiet streets at sunset. We found a vegan restaurant and were standing at the counter, gazing up at the menu board, trying to figure out what it all meant, when a male voice behind us said

hello in English-accented English.

We turned to see who it could be.

Boz Boorer!!!

"I was walking down the street," he said, "and I saw you two go in here, so I thought, I'll pop in and say hello."

Boz!!! We were so happy to see him!

We gave him hugs and he told us about how he'd

been walking up and down the street, trying to work up to handing his money over to one of the cambio merchants on the corner.

"Here I am, looking at one dodgy character after another, thinking, Naw!"

He told us about how he'd taken on the task of figuring out the exchange situation for all the lads, and he mentioned some of the details of the research he'd done that left me and my 'watch out for bad bills from taxi drivers' notes in the dust.

He was so funny, so friendly. We talked for a long time, took selfies with him, laughed at the bug situation on stage in Paraguay.

"There was one," Boz said, "flew right into the back of my head at the start of the clarinet solo for Paris. Right at that moment! It's not a long solo. But I kept playing, I didn't stop!"

We told him what a great show it was in Paraguay.

"Yeah," he agreed. "It was one of the best ones so far. It's amazing, they keep getting better and better."

"Absolutely," I said. "Really great."

Really great? Was that the best I could come up with? Boz was the co-writer of some of my favorite songs in the universe, one of my favorite musicians of all time. Was that all I had to say to him? But he was so down-to-earth, he really didn't invite gush.

"Yeah, I can see you enjoying it," he said.

Luckily, Nora stepped in and struck the right tone.

"Just in case you can't already tell," she said, "we think you're amazing."

He smiled and thanked us.

I think he got it.

The show at Teatro Opera was seated and luckily, we had front row seats. Well, true confession time, luck had nothing to do with it. When I'd gone to buy the tickets for this show as soon as they'd gone on sale, the website had rejected every single one of my credit cards, and I'd been forced to buy these tickets from a resale site. An unnameably large sum of money had changed hands, but I would never disclose it. These tickets were a surprise for Nora. Not a very special surprise given the fact that we'd ended up on the barrier at every show so far on the tour, but still. They were nothing to be sneezed at, especially given the fact that I had a letter to deliver to Morrissey.

We found Chayane in the crowd on the sidewalk outside the theater, and he introduced us to his local friends Pietro and Veronica.

"They had a dumb thing happen with their tickets," Chayane said. "They had front row seats, but the Morrissey crew had to remove the front row to put in a barrier, so they got moved."

"Row F," Veronica said, showing us her new ticket.

Oh no!

I confessed, and Veronica led us inside to the guy who would replace our tickets. He worked for the theater, and asked when I'd bought the tickets. I explained about the reseller and he asked how much I'd paid for them.

"Nora, could you please put your fingers in your ears?" I said, and told him the unnameably large sum.

He cussed really loud in Spanish.

"You don't have to go outside again," he said, when he handed us our new tickets. "You can wait here in the lobby until the doors open."

I felt kind of awful. Foolish for having been called out, having to say the unnameably large sum out loud. And kind of sick. Delivering the letter to Morrissey had seemed like a trivial detail with front-row seats. Now the little plastic bag in my hand felt like it had a lump of lead in it. Was I going to have to fight my way to the front to get rid of it?

But time passed, doors opened, and we walked in before the crowd arrived and not even glancing at our seats, strolled right up to the barrier to say hi to Trinity and then to Doug, another VIP who had arrived from the US to follow the rest of the tour. We parked ourselves beside Doug on the barrier, and had a lovely chat with him. Although Doug had been to hundreds of Morrissey shows, he was a very relaxed and modest person, and he talked about how much he appreciated each show individually on its own merits and how grateful he felt for them. Nora and I stayed right there at the barrier, unmolested by security, unquestioned by fans, and that was where we were when the show began.

I have a recurring fantasy that when I have something to deliver to Morrissey, I will hold it up during the line in Suedehead where he sings, "Why do you send me silly notes?" Seeing it, he'll come over immediately, pluck it out of my hand, job done, and on we go with the rest of the show.

At this show, Suedehead began and all of the delightful fans crushed into the space all around me sang the intro. It was so great, the stage was so close to the barrier, I could reach out and rest my hand on it. We were so close to Boz, the same Boz we'd talked to so recently! And here was my cue. Morrissey sang "Why do you send me silly notes?" I held my note up for him to see. He came over immediately. He stood directly in front of me. He reached down.

He shook Nora's hand as he sang the line, "I'm so sorry."

He didn't take my note.

Okay, that was how it was. I settled in for the long haul with my silly note. Chances were high it was going to be with me not just for the whole show, but for the subsequent walk to the nearest garbage can. Oh well. I wasn't going to let it ruin my night.

And really, it was quite a night.

Have I mentioned that every Morrissey show is different? That every one has its own unique flavor and essence?

This one was really fun, there was such a playful atmosphere. Morrissey was loose and free in his movements, gesturing big for emphasis, roaming around the stage, tossing the microphone cord here and there.

Recently, during Suedehead, he had pretty much always done a lyric substitution on the line, "You had to sneak into my room, just to read my diary." Sometimes he sang, "just to see the utter gloom." More often on this tour, he sang, "just to see too much

too soon." He did the too-much-too-soon substitution tonight, but then to my delight, he went on to the line, "It was just to see all the things you knew I'd written about you, and so many illustrations," and instead of illustrations, sang, "but so many empty pages."

Fun.

Alma Matters was, as always, fantastically received and sung by the audience with great gusto. It was such a warm and wonderful part of the South American shows, and this time, there was the extra sweetness of a stage invader. She was a young kid. Security tried to keep her back, but Morrissey reached out and helped her up on the stage and received her hug. She was quite overcome. She wasn't the only stage invader at that show. Later, again so sweetly, Morrissey reached out to a young

boy who came up and got his hug. He was far more gleeful than the girl, and when he was walking away, thought better of it, and ran back for a second squeeze.

The stage was quite small, so it was great to be able to see what drummer Matt Walker was up to. Nora and I were both learning how to play the drums, so everything Matt did behind the kit was super interesting to us. During the US tour, Nora had been trying to learn how to play Alma Matters, and she had stared so intently at him during that song at so many shows, the normally aloof Matt had finally caved, giving her a look that said, What?! What is it?! Why do you keep staring at me?!

How Soon Is Now? was super fun to watch Matt play, especially with the ending the song had now, where Matt gets up, whacks the giant gong that hangs behind him, then turns to the massive bass drum that stands beside it, and does the most thrilling electrifying solo, white strobe lights accentuating his every movement. Even as I was ready for it, even having seen it a number of times, I was freshly blown away by what I saw. He looked indomitable, like a drumming superhero.

And then I enjoyed watching him play First of the Gang, where no drumming heroics were required, just the ability to keep time with a shaker in his right hand while he drummed with his other limbs. The best part was when he would reach over and with a casual flick of the wrist, hit the crash with the shaker instead of a stick. (Talking about this later with Nora, she pointed out that from our perspective as beginning drummers, doing ANYTHING with your right hand while drumming with your other limbs definitely puts you in the category of drumming superhero, so I guess I take that back.)

Throughout the show, there were really entertaining exchanges between Morrissey and the audience. Before One of

Our Own, there were catcalls and cries of "I love you," from the audience.

"Yes, but do you mean it, though?" he asked.

The non-English-speaking audience was not quick enough to come back with a definitive response. There were a couple of faint cries of "Yes!"

"Two people answered!" Morrissey protested.

This drew a bigger response,

and a very distinct cry of "I love you!" from behind me to my left.

"Do you?" Morrissey said, looking in that direction. "Really? Aw!" He kept looking over there.

"What's your home address?" he said, then pretended to write on his hand. "What's your phone number?"

It was all very sweet and funny, but my favorite heckle of the night of course came from me, during Will Never Marry.

Morrissey started, softly singing the opening line, "I'm writing this to say, in a gentle way, thank you but no."

At this point he fell silent, and Jesse did the slide on his guitar than indicated that Morrissey was about to enter some kind of comedy routine around the song. (How does Jesse know when to do this? Is there a hand signal? Does he just intuit it?)

In the silence, there was laughter and applause from the audience.

"That's the end of the song!" Morrissey said, and without missing a beat, swung right into the second line, "I will live my life as I will undoubtedly die—"

Here he stopped singing abruptly, allowing the audience to sing the last word "alone!" loudly at him.

He stopped again to address the audience, correcting them firmly.

"I will not be alone," he said. "I will have my many animals."

At this point I was moved to interject.

"And me!" I shouted.

"My trees," he said.

"And me!" I reminded him.

"And even you!" he said, pointing in my direction.

I turned and did a mock swoon of delight over the barrier. But there really wasn't much that was mock about it. Morrissey'd said he'd have me. It was my lucky night!

There was something very warm and special about the whole night. Crashing Bores was particularly moving. It is one of my all-time favorite Morrissey songs because it captures the experience of the Four so succinctly. The Four is so alone, so misunderstood, surrounded by idiots—so lonely! "No one ever turns to me to say, take me in your arms, take me in your arms and love me!" Oh the poor Four! This song rings such deep resonant bells in my heart, it's ridiculous.

At this show, things were very snug on the barrier. As many people as humanly possible had squeezed in, and Nora and I were very cozy, facing each other, practically cheek to cheek.

And as the chorus of the song rolled around, and Nora and I put our arms around each other, I had the most delightful revelation.

This song was no longer about me.

Here I was, not just for now, but for always, held in the arms of the most loving, steadfast, true, intelligent, entertaining person I had ever met in my life. These arms holding me now were arms that would hold me any time I felt like being held, for the rest of my life.

I was loved.

Unequivocally. Unconditionally. Visibly and viscerally. The Four in me wanted to sing that same sad old lament, but how could I keep a straight face and sing about how neglected I was when I was kissing the love of my life on the neck?

I have mentioned this before, but it bears repeating at times like this:

I am very, very lucky.

The show moved to its inevitable conclusion with Let Me Kiss You. Morrissey again did the move where he ripped his shirt off on the line, "You open your eyes, and you see someone you physically despise." After he threw the shirt into the audience and left the stage, Boz, ever vigilant, strolled over to check out the shirt melee to make sure that everything was okay.

In the pause after the band left the stage, I looked at the letter I still held in my hand. Was it really destined for the trash? Yes. Definitely. I had done what I'd said I'd do. I had offered it to him, he'd seen it. He'd stood in front of me for whole songs, inches away from me, and hadn't taken it. I was going to have to take this rejection on the chin. I'd done everything a person could do, aside from leaping up on stage and stuffing it down his...

Hmmmm. Now that was an idea. The clock was ticking down the seconds. Why not go all out? What did I have to lose?

Morrissey and the band came back on stage and Morrissey took the microphone.

"Always trust your first instinct," he said. "Be kind to animals, look after your mother, but for God's sake, don't forget to live!"

Amen to that!

And so began The Queen Is Dead! Yes! My favorite song to attempt stage invasions to!

But oh! Two security guards were on me before I could even begin. In my usual style, I refused to give up, even with all the odds against me. The security guard pinning down my right shoulder was really quite a gentleman. He kept saying things to me in a very reasonable tone. Very reasonable things, I'm sure, but I couldn't understand them because they were in Spanish. I really warmed to him during the few minutes we had together. To show him how I meant no harm, I looked into his eyes and sang to him.

"So I broke into the palace, with a sponge and a rusty spanner. She said, I know you and you cannot sing. I said, That's nothing, you should hear me play pianner!"

Morrissey came by, of course, every now and then, to stand right in front of my flailing letter-waving self, and—why break the habit of a whole show?—walk away without taking it.

I wasn't going to give up, no way no how. We were heading into the final seconds of the song. Morrissey wasn't walking around anymore. He had situated himself in front of the microphone stand to sing the last, lonesome lines, "Life is very long when you're lonely."

And—wonder of wonders—after one "Life is very long when you're lonely," he came over, took my letter, slipped it into his back pocket, and was back at the microphone in time to sing the next.

Done. It was done. The show was done. Everything was done. It was time to go.

And get up the next morning to get on line for the show at Luna Park.

The most notable thing about our day on line at Luna Park was Nora's bag getting stolen! We were sitting on a heavily trafficked sidewalk, near a bus stop where the Morrissey queue was mingling with the line for the bus. People constantly walked past us, and one of them stopped and asked me what time it was.

I couldn't say the numbers in Spanish, so I showed him my watch. He looked at it for an inordinately long time. How hard could it be to read the time? Really!

But of course it was all a ruse. While our attention was on him, his friend had sneaked up behind Nora and taken her bag. She didn't notice until they were long gone. There was nothing valuable in it.

"Just my notebook," she said glumly. "I guess I won't be much help to you writing your book."

The bag she had left in the taxi in São Paulo had also had her notebook. This was the replacement, where she'd written about the shows we'd seen since then. I had my notebook with me too, to write about the previous night's show before the memories got overwritten by the next one.

"Just don't go losing yours," Nora said. "Or you'll really be screwed."

The day was so busy, meditating, writing, eating, talking with Alyssa and Juli, a Brazilian fan we'd met in Brasilia. When we got to doors, it was clear we were going to make the barrier

(again, for the tenth time!) and Nora asked what side I wanted to aim for.

"The Jesse side, please," I said. "I really need to spend some time with Jesse."

In Asunción, Jesse's solos had rung out with extra flair and passion, and I'd made the plan to study him up close as soon as I could. At the show the previous night, we'd ended up on the Boz side because we were talking to Doug, but tonight we were going to get a chance to take in some Jesse guitar magic.

I was really looking forward to it, even though I am not one of nature's guitarists. I know this because at one point, I really gave it a good try. As a singer, it's a really good idea to be able to accompany yourself on guitar, so I really did my best to learn how to play. I took group classes, individual lessons. I practiced for an hour every day. I worked with three different teachers. I played at recitals, open mics. I kept waiting for the part where I would stop sounding like absolute crap, but that day never dawned. At the end of two years, I sounded just as awful to my own ears as I did on day one, so I allowed myself to quit. These days, I accompany myself on piano or drums, instruments that forgive beginners their crude ignorance, allowing me to feel happy about playing music, even if I'm not very good at it.

So whatever it takes to play the guitar, I know I don't have it. But two years of trying like mad has given me an increased appreciation of what real guitarists actually do, even when the level at which they play is way beyond anything I could ever have mastered.

When we made it inside, Nora, Juli and I ended up on the Jesse side, right in front of the spot where he would come forward to do his solos. Perfect.

The venue was really big. A lot of the bigger venues on this tour had been outdoor, but this massive crowd was housed indoors. The videos came on, and Nora and I watched for the audience's reaction to the Ding Dong the Witch Is Dead segment on Margaret Thatcher. She was the Prime Minister who had been in power when England and Argentina had gone to war over the Falkland Islands, so it was fair to guess that she was probably not Argentina's favorite politician. There hadn't been much of a reaction to the video the night before, but tonight, with a much larger crowd than there had been in the theater, there was a very definite boo-and-hiss that rose up, and laughter at the final shot in the video:

At this point in the tour, I had experienced the wonderful phenomenon that was the South American audience many times. As the videos came to a close and dramatic music filled the darkened stage, heralding Morrissey's arrival, I could feel it happening again. The crowd gelled, their voices raised in whoops and cheers, and the whole room's energy coalesced. We were all ourselves still, but now also part of the single beast that was the audience for this show. And this massive beast filling all of Luna Park, what an energy it had! Morrissey and the band appeared, the band in black button-down shirts, Morrissey in white, and they faced each other and did their customary bow. Before he began Suedehead, Morrissey sang a capella (to the tune of the opening couplet of America from *West Side Story*): "Argentina, my heart's devotion, never sink into the ocean."

It was ridiculous. It was great. The crowd loved it.

Suedehead began and wow, the crowd sang as one (they sang the intro too, of course). As Morrissey prowled the stage asking us the perennial question, "Why do you come here?" he occasionally came forward to the edge of the stage. Whenever he did, the screaming in the audience ramped up and there was a push to the front, arms reaching, fans doing their best to get to touch him even for a second. It didn't feel at all rough or dangerous, it had the good-natured affectionate feeling that Morrissey hysteria had in this part of the world.

A few lucky fans got their handshakes during Suedehead and during the beginning of the next song, Alma Matters. And then—his proximity always electrifying—Morrissey came over to our side of the stage. He reached down and shook hands with Juli beside me, who apologized to me later for holding on to Morrissey's hand for so long. (Why did people apologize for things that were extremely normal behaviors at Morrissey concerts: clinging to Morrissey's hand, bawling their eyes out etc.?)

And then after Juli released his hand, he turned his attention to me.

I'd been blindsided by the handshake I'd gotten in Brasilia. Why me? Why now? But this one was not a surprise. It was about the letter I'd given him the night before. Morrissey was no ordinary pen pal. On the plus side, one of the most talented and intelligent human beings on the planet had read a letter I wrote to him—magic! On the downside, he wasn't much for writing back, so there was no way to know how it was received. Was it at all the right thing, or was it just another irritating intrusion from a fan? Here he was, reaching out his hand to me. This was my answer. It was a really good feeling to shake Morrissey's hand under any circumstances, but under these circumstances, it felt especially good. I gave his hand a firm shake, and happy happy happy, on we went with the rest of the show.

When I'd bought tickets for this show, Google-translated comments for the event had literally translated the word 'Luna' and presented me with frequent updates that began with the words, "On Dec 10, Morrissey will appear on the moon..." And it was true. The band was so fantastically fit, Morrissey in such good voice, they had managed to reach escape velocity and were giving us a show that was out of this world.

They launched into This Charming Man, a song that just got better and better every time they played it. They followed it with First of the Gang, and Morrissey, as he had frequently done on this tour, stood at the microphone and led the audience, clapping his hands in a steady beat for the whole song. I think everyone in the whole place sang, jumped, clapped along in time together. The band responded, coming back with an extra spring in every note they played. It was playful, wonderful, so full of happiness.

And Jesse? I was so happy that we were standing right in front of him, getting to watch up close as he came forward to the edge of the stage to do his solos.

I could never sing like Morrissey did, never play the drums or keyboard like Matt or Gustavo, but at least I understood from my own experience how they were doing it. But Jesse?

Where was he going when he reached inside himself to find that solo? How was that sound coming to be? It was such a mystery.

And it wasn't just the solos. I found my eye drawn to Jesse more and more as the show went on. He was doing something really special, the sound coming from his guitar had such an amazing tone. Each song had a saturated, vibrant feel that conjured a sense that we were hearing a favorite classic, even the songs from the new album. Each one evoked a feeling of, Yes, this is it, this is how music is supposed to sound. It was so full, so satisfying, it had a hint of nostalgia built into it. These were the golden days, these were our favorite songs, this night would live forever in our hearts.

Since I'm a fan who's jumped on board the Morrissey train so late in the game, I sometimes wonder what it would be like if I'd found him sooner. What amazing show would I go back in time to see? What era of Morrissey's career would be the ideal one to catch? What legendary tour was the best one?

As I watched Morrissey sing song after song, from the classic How Soon Is Now? through Crashing Bores and Ganglord, up to the most recent favorite Kiss Me a Lot, I knew with 100% certainty that this was it. The best time was right now. The legendary tour that nobody would want to miss was South America 2015.

Everyday Is Like Sunday was again extra special, massively wistful, beautiful.

"Share some grease tea with me, por favor," Morrissey sang in the final verse as he made his way over to our side of the stage.

For this whole tour, in the final moments of the song, he had improvised a beautiful ending to the repeated words, "More grist for the mill." I'd heard it so often, it had become a part of the song for me, so I began singing it as usual, but Morrissey was doing something else, a different melody, fewer words. I proceeded to sing the "More grist for the mill," part anyway as he sang the other line. It went together perfectly and I ended up singing a spontaneous and harmonious duet with Morrissey that only I could hear. Perfect.

When the song ended, there was shouting, chanting from the crowd.

"Por qué?" Morrissey asked playfully. "Problem?"

He walked over to the front of the stage where, of course, there were dozens of hands reaching up to him, one of them proffering a piece of paper. He took the piece of paper, unfolded it, read it as he walked back to the microphone, then folded it again.

"No problem now," he pronounced. Then he proceeded to introduce The Bullfighter Dies, a song where there was a very big problem for the bull in Spain.

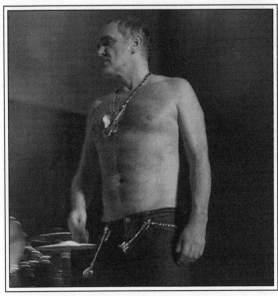

The show moved on, and I wanted it to never stop, but we got to the point where he sang Let Me Kiss You, ripped off his shirt, tossed it into the audience and left the stage. But no, the band didn't follow him. He came back a moment later in a fresh shirt and sang one more song,

I Will See You in Far Off Places, prefacing it with the words, "I give you my prayers of thanks. Thank you for listening, and I love you more than life."

The encore was The Queen Is Dead and every word, every note rang out so deliciously, how could anyone want it to end? Morrissey had picked up an Argentinian flag that someone had thrown on the stage, and was waving it around as he sang, tossing it gracefully from one hand to the other. He sang the last, "Life is very long when you're lonely," but didn't leave the stage. As the band completed their final big flourish, he took the microphone once more.

"I loff you!" he said. "I loff you!"

He said it again. He said it, I don't know, maybe a million times, holding the flag aloft in a moment that really could not, should not end. But finally he covered his face and head with the flag and walked off the stage and the final delicious, resonant note of the show rang out, and it was over.

Nora and I talked about it later, talked about how incredibly lucky we were to be at a show that was one of the best Morrissey had ever played. We talked too about my now-favorite guitar player in the world, Jesse Tobias.

Looking up Jesse's Wikipedia page, we learned that he'd worked with one of our favorite writers, Joss Whedon. I was into his later work, but Nora was a big Buffy the Vampire Slayer fan, and was excited to learn that he was involved in producing the wildly awesome Buffy musical episode. It was good to learn more about Jesse, to get a sense of where he was coming from musically.

"But do you know what has been most useful in helping me understand Jesse?" Nora said. "The pictures of the guitar players with the giant slugs."

Yes, she was right. Taking another look at the Slug Solos Tumblr feed, it was clear that guitar players were going through

something incomprehensible to outsiders in the process of making those fantastic sounds. But yes, picturing them holding a giant slug while they did it really helped.

DECEMBER 17, 2015
TEATRO DE VERANO
MONTEVIDEO, URUGUAY

Our next show wasn't a Morrissey gig, it was something that had been around for a lot longer. On the border between Argentina and Brazil, flowing through the middle of the jungle, there is a river called the Iguazu. And on that river there is a place where the water takes a magnificent dive, thundering down to create a spectacular waterfall. It doesn't do this in just one

spot, there is a whole complex of falls, from picturesque cascades to beasts so massive, the plume of mist rising off them can be seen for miles around. When Eleanor Roosevelt first saw Iguazu, she was reported to have exclaimed, "Poor Niagara!"

There was so much to see at Iguazu, we spent two full days there, and still didn't get to see it all.

There was one spot where we stopped and stood for a while, letting the waterfall speak to us, letting it reveal over time what it had to show. We were there for quite a while before Nora exclaimed, "It's a lizard!" and the bumpy protuberance on top of the rock right in

front of my eyes stopped being just a gray lump and showed what it really was.

The lizard rock was right in front of the best spot to take self-ies, and for the next 20 minutes or so, we watched an endless parade of people take pictures of themselves beside the lizard. None of them noticed that he was there.

The hotel we were staying at, the Sheraton Iguazu, was fan-tastic. It was the only hotel in Iguazu National Park, we were surrounded by jungle on all sides. And we all know who lives in the jungle.

El mono.

Our first sighting was very soon after we arrived. Sitting in the hotel room, I could hear a child shrieking excitedly in Span-ish.

"El mono en la habitación! El mono en la habitación!"

Idly, I pieced it together, quite pleased with myself that I was able to translate this sentence. Habitación meant hotel room. And el mono was a—

I leapt up.

"There's a monkey in that kid's hotel room!" I said to Nora and we dashed out onto the balcony to see the monkey fleeing

the scene, climbing up the side of the building up to-wards the roof.

Of course that wasn't the end of it. The next morning, while we waited for a heavy rainstorm to pass, we stood on the balcony and watched the show.

Out in front of us, there was a mesh awning that gave shelter to a driveway below.

This awning was bouncy, flexible, and monkeys, I don't know, maybe a dozen of them, ran back and forth on it, bouncing along like it was a trampoline.

The rain was a soaking downpour, but it didn't put the slightest dent in their exuberant play. They jumped, ran, tumbled, gave each other piggyback rides.

This was our third time seeing monkeys on the trip. We'd seen the weirdly wizened-faced marmosets near Sugarloaf, and then the monkeys swinging in the trees of Parque Lage in Rio. But this time, watching their endless, tireless play, I felt I finally caught the gist of monkeydom, could really appreciate what they were saying to me.

"I'm a monkey and I love it!" was the song they sang in their play. "Being a monkey is fun fun fun!"

And then of course there were the coatis, raccoon-like animals that wandered all around. Baby coatis are way up there on the cuteness scale, just FYI.

There was so much to see, but all too soon, it was time to pack our bags again and get ready to fly to Montevideo for the next-to-last show of the tour. Everything I'd worn at Iguazu was sopping wet, soaked through by the spray from the falls. I spent the last evening ironing clothes, trying to dry them out, running a hairdryer through my only pair of sneakers, but I didn't make much progress. I felt defeated by all of the water, exhausted. I wondered if I was coming down with something as I got into bed. Something was definitely a bit off.

Water, water everywhere. I kept waking up every half-hour to pee, and kept dreaming about water. By midnight it was clear I had a urinary tract infection. By 3am, things had gotten quite a bit worse. I could feel a growing pain in my kidneys, and there was blood visible in my urine.

Crap!

I was sick, really properly sick. I wasn't going to make it to the Montevideo show. We were leaving in the morning, and I was clearly in no shape to get on a plane. We were going to have to reschedule the flight, I wouldn't make it to the show, and would probably end up making Nora miss it too. Everything was ruined!

I just wanted to roll up in a ball and cry.

But I couldn't. I just wouldn't let myself do it. This was a Morrissey show that was waiting for me. I couldn't just flush it down the drain. There had to be a way. I wasn't going to give up.

"Think," I told myself. "Stop feeling sorry for yourself and think. Solve this problem. How can you make it work?"

Okay, I thought, If I start taking antibiotics right now, in the middle of the night, maybe I'll be well enough to travel by mid-morning. Then, at the very least, we'll make it to Montevideo and even if I'm stuck in bed, Nora won't miss the show.

I woke Nora up.

"I'm sick," I said, and explained to her how I needed antibiotics ASAP. She went down to the front desk to ask them how I could get some.

"You can wait until 8am and go see the doctor," she said when she got back. "Or you can go to the Emergency Room right now. They'll call you a taxi."

"Okay," I said, "let's go."

We got in a taxi and left the national park and drove through the utterly deserted streets of Puerto Iguazu. The hospital was tiny. I was the only patient in the Emergency Room. I was led straight away into the examination room. Nobody got me to fill out any forms. A nurse handed me a thermometer and I put it in my mouth.

She covered her mouth in horror, and mimed putting the thermometer under her arm.

Oh that was how they did things here. Oops.

The doctor came in and asked me about my symptoms, started probing my abdomen.

"Does this hurt?" she said, poking at my kidneys.

"Yes!" I said.

Asking for my passport, she wrote my name and passport number on a prescription for antibiotics and pain medication. And that was it. Fifteen minutes after we'd arrived, we were back in the taxi. It was so odd to walk out of there without presenting at least a credit card.

Our taxi driver was a very thorough guy. I thought he was kind of nuts when he did the rounds of Puerto Iguazu, stopping at every pharmacy and jumping out to see if they were open. It's 4am, buddy, I felt like saying, let it go.

But finally we stopped at a closed-looking pharmacy that had someone inside, and Nora passed the prescription through the slot over the door and voilà, there were my antibiotics and pain meds.

"It cost less than twenty US dollars," Nora said. "It's almost like they want sick people to get well in this country."

We got back to the hotel less than an hour after we'd set out.

The guy behind the desk insisted that the hotel pick up the tab for the taxi.

Less than twenty dollars for a visit to the ER? We were clearly a very, very long way from home.

By morning I was feeling better. Not all-the-way better, but just about better enough to get on a plane. It all went fine. We caught our flight to Buenos Aires, and made our connection to the ferry to Montevideo. When we got off the boat, we caught a taxi to the hotel, and I finally made it to our room and crawled into bed.

Montevideo!

It was quite likely that I wasn't going to see anything more of the city than this hotel room, so I asked Nora to leave the curtains open so I could take in the view. And really it was an amazing view. The top attraction of Montevideo was the Rambla, a long walking and biking path that ran alongside the huge Rio de la Plata that hugged Montevideo on three sides. Our hotel was a block away from the Rambla. From our vantage point on a high floor, we could see the late evening sun lighting the big sky. The river beneath it seemed to stretch out into forever. Even though I probably wasn't going to make it to the show, I felt amazed and grateful. In spite of a really virulent infection, we'd made it here with the minimum amount of fuss and disruption. It felt kind of miraculous.

The next day was a day of rest. I sent Nora out to buy me food and vitamins and massive bottles of water I drank all day to help clear the infection out of my system. By evening I wondered if maybe I would be able to make it to the show the next day after all. I decided to test my strength, and we walked down the Rambla to the venue to check it out.

How lovely Montevideo was! I was so glad to get out and see some of it. The venue was just off the Rambla, it was an outdoor theater with an ornate band shell covering the stage, and benches

for the audience to sit on. A perfect setup for a place called Teatro de Verano—the Summer Theater. There was a beach across the street, and we went and sat for a while, watching people swimming and playing as an amazing sunset lit up the massive sky. When it got dark, we walked to a nearby vegan restaurant for an excellent lentil curry that fed my growing suspicion that Montevideo was a truly wonderful place to live.

I wanted to see more, but my strength was flagging. We got in a taxi and went back to the hotel.

"I can make it to the show," I told Nora. "But only if I spend the day in bed. I just don't have the strength to be on line all day. I don't mind being in the back."

"Okay," Nora said. "But maybe we could get you to the front. Why don't you come and get on the list in the morning and then go back to the hotel and rest after that?"

"I don't know," I said. "I'll see how I feel in the morning."

When we woke up the next morning, it looked like our good luck had run out. Nora opened the curtains and we looked out on a truly dismal sight. The sky was stuffed with ferocious thunderclouds that were releasing immense amounts of rain onto the iron-gray river beneath, gusts of wind were smashing raindrops onto the window. The forecast said thunderstorms all day long, continuing into the night. Summer theater, indeed. There was no way the show could go on.

"I'm not even getting out of bed," I said to Nora, and rolled over and went back to sleep.

But Nora, undaunted, suited up in her rain gear and went out to wait on line.

She wasn't the only one. Text updates from her reported that there was indeed a line. The summer theater was very exposed,

there wasn't any shelter but Alyssa and the South American fans were there, undaunted. Nora reported that they were hopping over the fence to a more sheltered spot. Then another text saying they were being chased out by security. Then back over the fence again. She sounded quite cheerful.

But the texts turned grim in the early afternoon. There was a rumor going around that the show was definitely canceled, the official announcement was going to be made any minute.

"I'm coming back to the hotel," Nora texted.

That was it. Montevideo was a bust. The show couldn't be postponed until tomorrow, the Lima show was the day after that. It was no longer a show day. Time to let Montevideo go and turn our thoughts to Lima.

But no! My heart rebelled! I refused to let it go!

Really? Was I so spoiled that having seen Morrissey ten times in a row, I was going to throw a tantrum because show number eleven was canceled?

No, it wasn't quite like that. It was something deeper. Something very beautiful and moving was developing and deepening in my heart because of these shows. This tour was the most prolonged and powerful heart-opening experience I'd ever had. Hearing that the show was canceled, the temptation was for the heart to shut up like a clam shell, to protect itself from the hurt of a disappointed wish.

But what if the heart stayed open? I had fought my way to Montevideo, defeated the watery curse of my dreadful infection, only to be defeated now by this watery deluge from the heavens. Could I stand it?

Can you stay open? I asked my heart. Can you be here with what is?

Yes, my heart said. On one condition. As long as this continues being a show day. As long as nobody gives up on this show, no matter what happens, no matter what anybody says, even if it's canceled.

This seemed like an odd request for the rational mind to process, but I went with it.

Okay, I said, this is a show day. No matter what.

Illogical as it was, there was a really deep wisdom in the heart's request. How often did I let myself really feel the feeling of wanting something that I absolutely could not have? Can't have what you want? Then shut the whole heart down! That was my usual approach. But the idea of leaving this a show day even though the show had been removed kept my heart open. The feeling of wanting the show to still be there pierced my heart. This was a show day, so lots of meditation was in order, and I sat with the feeling, nurturing my heart in the judgement-free space of awareness.

It was about this time that the rain stopped.

Nora came back, took off her rain gear, got into bed beside me.

"I just wish they'd make the official announcement," she said. "Then I could let it go."

But time passed and more time passed and the announcement wasn't made.

"That's it," Nora said. "I'm going back to the line."

I looked at my phone. The forecast said it was going to be dry for the next couple of hours, but then the storm would ramp up again after 6pm. It predicted 100% chance of rain at showtime. I wished Nora luck.

As I continued my afternoon of meditation, I focused particularly on sending loving kindness towards the person whose job it was to make the judgement call of whether the show should be canceled or not. Sure, it was dry now, but what kind of mess would it be to start the show and then abandon it three songs in because of a downpour? And how much worse would it be to cancel the show and then have the forecast clear up, blue skies for the rest of the day? As the hours wore on, I saw that whoever this person was, they had decided to postpone making the judgement call until the last possible minute, hoping that the forecast would shift.

It didn't shift. At 6pm, it still said 100% chance of rain at showtime.

My heart was open. I was going to fully have this experience, no matter how painful it was. I wasn't going to hide out in my room, avoiding the bad news. I got dressed and packed my raincoat and set off down the Rambla to the venue. I was going to be there with my peeps when the ax fell. And it would still be a show day, no matter what.

Have I mentioned already that the early-evening light in Montevideo is a wonder to behold? It hadn't rained all afternoon and now the clouds were breaking up, the sun streaming through in rays of celestial light. The air was still and warm, there wasn't a puff of wind. Walking down the Rambla to the venue was like taking a walk to Heaven. Every step I took, every curve of the winding path, the weather became more and more beautiful.

Was I dreaming? Was this real? Could it be true?

I arrived at the venue and looked out over the beach, the tiny wispy remaining clouds and the warm sun gearing up to make another spectacular Montevideo sunset, and I accepted the truth that my heart had known all day long. This was a show day no matter what. I took out my phone. It still said 100% chance of rain at showtime. I looked at the deep blue sky, the last clouds melting away even as I looked.

I found Nora who had just picked up our tickets at the ticket window and hugged her.

"I can't believe it," I said. "Look at the weather! It's a miracle!"

"I know!" she said.

She led me to the line and presented me to the list administrator who wrote '15' on my hand and I took my place beside Nora and Elina who also had '15' written on their hands. This was how this list was administered in Montevideo, you could write down not only your own name, but hold spaces for your friends by writing their names down too. The list was administered so strictly in other parts of the world, this felt almost like some kind of treason, but I accepted it for what it was. It was more of the miracle. Nothing was going to stop me from seeing this show, apparently. Not the hell of a urinary tract infection, not the high water of a 100%-chance-of-rain thunderstorm. I was here no matter what.

Doors opened and I took my place on the barrier beside Nora, Chayane and Elina. The barrier was curved, miles away from the stage, and much lower than it. The gulf between stage and audience was massive. There would be no handshakes tonight. The pre-show videos played and I was so conscious of the fact that this was the next-to-last time that I would see these videos. The day after tomorrow was the show in Lima, and then it was all over. Charles Aznavour appeared on the screen and sang his bittersweet song of heart's longing, "Emmenez-moi au bout de la terre..."

I looked around me. The sun had set at this point, and just to the left of the stage, a crescent moon was hanging low in the cloudless sky. With the curved barrier, I had to turn my head just a little to the right to see all the faces of the audience lit up by the reflected light from the screen. These were my people. The faces of my new friends from North and South America shone out bright among the crowd, but I could feel the warmth that connected all of us—every single person in that summer theater felt like they were a part of my heart.

The stage was all set up. Soon Morrissey and the band would appear. Charles Aznavour sang on, his heart pierced with longing for everything he didn't have, but I didn't feel an answering pang of longing in my heart. I was complete. This was my place. Right here at the barrier, this was it. Somehow, I had been delivered to the land of marvels again. It happened over and over again on this tour. It was really a miracle.

The show began and before Suedehead, Morrissey said, "Montevideo, I come here to spill my heart!"

Oh, I could feel my heart opening like a flower to the music, the rich delicacy of the contact with each note. And oh, behind me and Nora, two merrily drunk local lads, tall and long-armed, pushed their way to the front, and arrived right behind us. Their hairy arms reached past our faces to punch the air for emphasis on the chorus of Suedehead: "I'm! so! sorry!" They sang right in our ears, super loud, heavily accented, wildly out of key. Nora and I looked at each other and grinned. These guys with their puppy dog exuberance were great. Montevideo was great. South America was great. Morrissey was great. Everything was as it should be.

And so again, the show unfolded. After Suedehead, there was Alma Matters, Speedway and Ganglord. The same songs, but of course, different, because every Morrissey show was different, every show had its own distinct essence and flavor.

However, this time, the difference was really highlighted by my experience of the bass.

Throughout the tour, Nora had asked me a recurring question after each show.

"Did you remember to listen to Mando?"

And I always had to smack my forehead and say, "No!"

Nora had bought a bass and had found the time to squeeze in one bass lesson before we left on our trip. I think this had tuned her ear to the instrument, because after shows, she kept pointing out details of what Mando's playing had been like.

"You have to listen to him during Meat Is Murder," she'd said. "He and Matt Walker are the most perfect unit of rhythmic excellence."

Well this time, I remembered to pay attention to him right from the start. It felt odd to have my eyes on him, he didn't invite scrutiny. He was the most self-effacing member of the band. He stood in the back, never had a reason to come to the front for solos like Boz or Jesse or Gustavo, wasn't playing a big shiny drum kit like Matt. Mando kept his eyes on the floor, simply getting on with the business of playing the bass. He was there to make music, not to be looked at.

But I looked. And noticed things. He was wearing the same cheap plastic Casio watch that I was wearing. Had he read Trip-Advisor too, and was trying to throw pickpockets off the scent by wearing a cheap watch? Or was he wearing it because frankly cheap plastic Casio watches are kind of awesome?

I noticed that the watch was on his left hand. Which was the hand that he was playing the bass with. And that triggered a blindingly obvious realization: Mando was left-handed!

What kind of witchery did Morrissey perform? How did he soak up so much of our attention? Mando's bass was pointing in the opposite direction to Boz and Jesse's guitars. It was so obvious. It was incredible that I hadn't noticed it until now.

It reminded me of a conversation I'd had with Nora earlier in the tour where I said, "You know the part of Far Off Places where Gustavo comes to the front of the stage and dances around playing the accordion?" and Nora'd looked puzzled and said, "Gustavo plays the accordion?" That was the attention-magnet Morrissey was. If he was singing, or even just standing around playing the maracas, was there anything else even worth noticing?

The answer to that of course was, Yes! I kept my eye on Mando, really listened to what he was doing, and that triggered another blindingly obvious realization. It was one I had repeatedly, song after song, and it went something like this.

"This song has a bass line!"

It was so fantastic. With my eye on Mando and my ear finally tuned to the bass, I was taking in a new dimension of each of these songs. I loved these songs so much already, and now a new facet of them was being presented for me to enjoy. It was quite exquisite. And Nora was right, Mando was amazing. He and Matt Walker were utterly in sync, locked tight, rhythmic excellence indeed.

The night was so lovely, the air was so still, the moon was shining above us all in the sky. There was a special feeling about the show. Special that it was happening at all—a victory snatched from the jaws of rainy defeat. But special too because it was happening here in this lovely city, with this warm audience, people whose hearts had longed, I'm sure, as vehemently as mine for the rain to stop and their dream of seeing Morrissey to come true.

Odd as the setup was, with the curved barrier holding us so far back from the stage, it didn't take anything away from the night.

Morrissey said something like, "I am happy to play here in this heart-shaped country," at one point. A deep and wide gulf was not enough to stop the connection from happening.

Morrissey even used the deep gulf for some visual humor. When he sang I'm Throwing My Arms Around Paris, on the "in the absence of human touch" line, he bent down and groped towards the nearest human, a security guard who was standing in the gulf. But the gulf was so far below the stage, the security guard was oblivious to the arm groping far above his head. It was quite striking.

Morrissey even stopped to talk about it between songs. He pointed out the fact that everywhere you go, there is a gulf that divides.

There was a chorus of shouts in response to this. Including mine.

"You're all talking at once!" he protested.

"Come down here!" I suggested, pointing to the gulf.

It was a conversation I'd had with Elina earlier that made me think of it. Seeing the setup, she'd reminisced about a show she'd been to in England, a festival where Morrissey had come down into the gulf to shake hands with fans.

He saw what I was suggesting and with a very dubious look on his face, shook his head.

"Okay," I shrugged.

He was probably right. If he got down into the gulf, it could trigger an incident, fans swarming over the barrier like fish over a dam. He was better off where he was.

And where he was, it was really perfect. The audience was perfect too, singing along so happily to favorites like How Soon Is Now? and This Charming Man. First of the Gang was particularly enthusiastically received (a song that Morrissey introduced by saying in a very solemn tone, "I'd like to dedicate this next song to Hector, who died this week.") I should have been used to it by now, but it still tickled me so much to hear the audience singing the intro along to Jesse's guitar. Everyone sang, clapped, bounced along in time to the music. It was all wonderful.

There was something about the curved barrier—something that had looked like such an impediment at first glance—that felt very right. It formed a half-circle of fans that joined and came together with the half-circle of Morrissey and the band standing on stage. This full circle that we described echoed the completeness of this magic tour, determined to play out its full circuit. It brought a feeling of unity to the show. Everyone was them-

selves, standing in their own space, playing their part, and yet at the same time, everyone was an integral and beautiful part of the whole. The band played I Will See You In Far Off Places, and the harmonious circle we were standing in allowed space to notice everything: guitars, drums, Mando's amazing bass line, Morrissey pointing into the depths of the gulf as he sang about seeing us in far off places, even Gustavo coming to the front to dance around as he played the accordion.

After Meat Is Murder (where Mando really played an incredible bass line I had never noticed before!) Morrissey came out in a gorgeous shirt with flowers on it. It went wonderfully with the white rosary necklace he'd been wearing all night. I was struck anew by the sheer beauty of him, framed so perfectly by this shirt, by this band, by this show, by this night. We all played our parts in this whole, and he was the heart of it, always, the tender point of contact and connection.

"Close your eyes," he sang, "and think of someone you physically admire, and let me kiss you, let me kiss you."

At the end of the song, he tossed the beautiful shirt into

the audience and left the stage. After he was gone, as the last lines of the music played, Jesse came over to the Boz side and they stood at the front of the stage, playing their guitars, checking out the shirt melee.

Jesse tossed a pick at us, a nice gesture for sure, but with us in the front row, how could it not end up lost in the depths of the gulf? I made a face at Jesse, like, better luck next time. But then I saw that Nora was reaching under the barrier. The pick had landed on a ledge right in front of her and she was able to retrieve it. A minute later, a second one landed two inches from where the first had been, so we got one each.

Morrissey's emerged for the encore wearing another beautiful shirt. This one was similar to the first, but had pink flowers instead of blue ones. He sang The Queen Is Dead, and threw the shirt into the audience to be ripped to pieces at the end of the song.

"I love you!" he yipped into the microphone before leaving the stage, and even as we all dispersed and went our separate ways (eventually! South American audiences were very reluctant to leave) there was a sense of carrying something away from the night. The fans who left clutching a precious piece of flowered fabric walked away with a tangible reminder of it. But I'd like to think that we all carried it with us somehow, that sense of unity, that we'd all been brought together in that circle, woven into something bigger and more beautiful than ourselves on this precious night, when the moon had miraculously shone down on us from a beautiful clear and cloudless sky.

DECEMBER 19, 2015
PARQUE DE LA EXPOSICION
LIMA, PERU

The end was speeding towards us faster than we could believe. We didn't even get a full night's sleep after the Montevideo show. We had to be up at 4am to catch our 6:20am flight to Lima. It was the only direct flight from Montevideo to Lima that day, so we ran into Alyssa, Elina and Trinity as soon as we arrived in the airport. And then when we got to the gate, after we'd settled down in a nearby café to eat, Alyssa nodded her head towards the line that was forming as pre-boarding was announced.

"It's Boz and Gustavo and Matt," she said.

I looked over my shoulder. Fantastic. I'd really hoped I'd get to meet Matt Walker before the tour was over, and here was my big chance.

"I'm going to go ask for their autographs," I said. "Are you guys coming?"

Alyssa was very careful about not crossing boundaries when it came to Morrissey and the band, and Nora probably would have come with me if it wasn't still the middle of the night, her presence maybe seen as an irritating intrusion.

I was on my own. No problem.

Boz and Gustavo were happy to see me again—Gustavo even remembered my name, how sweet!—and I think Matt was fine with meeting me too. He wasn't at all fazed by being hugged twice and being told that he was beautiful. That order of business taken care of, we got down to talking about music. I told him that I really appreciated watching him play because I too played the drums. The enormity of the difference in our skill level reared up in my mind, and I quickly had to qualify that statement.

"Just a little bit," I said. "I'm just a beginner."

"Yeah me too," he said. "I play the drums just a little bit."

He seemed so nice, it was dreadful that Nora was missing this. I was beginning to work on him, trying to get him to come over to where Nora was sitting to say hi, but she saved me by walking up and joining the conversation.

"Great show last night," she said.

"And it almost didn't happen," I added.

"I know!" Gustavo said. "We were on stage doing sound check, and they kept saying, Hurry up, hurry up, it's going to rain! And while we were standing there, the sun broke through the clouds, this beam of sunlight shone right in my eyes, and I was like, Oh, it's a sign!"

The sun shining down on the magic tour. And here was more magic, standing around chatting with these lovely, lovely guys like we were old pals, Boz telling funny stories about all the flights he'd missed over the years. The enchantment just never stopped.

After we got on the plane, a schmaltzy Christmas song came on over the speakers, something in the "Santa Baby" genre and I turned to Nora.

"Oh, you should have told Gustavo about that funny dream you had!" I said. "The one where he put out a Christmas album!"

Vexed by the fact that even in South America, we couldn't avoid hearing the same six crappy Christmas songs that played on the radio at home, Nora had talked—and then dreamed— about the ideal solution: a Christmas album written by Gustavo. It would be super tasteful, with lots of flamenco guitar, sleigh bells, spare lyrics in Spanish, and maybe even a hint of pan pipes, to bring in that Andean flair.

"I did tell him!" Nora said. "I even described the album cover, where he was in a sweater in front of a fire, maybe in a ski lodge, and wearing a little Santa hat."

"Did he get the concept?" I said, laughing. "Do you think he'll do it?"

"I don't think so," Nora said. "He was polite. But puzzled."

Our plane landed in Lima at 9am, and back at home, when making the itinerary for this trip, I'd penciled in the possibility of visiting a pyramid later in the day. We had come full circle, Peru was next door to where the tour had begun in Ecuador, so we were back in the beautiful land of the Andes, Incas, pan pipes and El Condor Pasa. Huaca Huallamarca was a huge ancient pyramid, right in the middle of Lima, and looking at the map back home, it had seemed like a very simple thing to sneak a quick visit in late in the afternoon, something I could do by myself if Nora wasn't interested.

But it turned out that reality was very different to a map, and Lima was not the kind of town you wandered around on your own. Our hotel was in the middle of the oldest part of town, chosen for its proximity to the venue. But this historical downtown was not like others we'd seen on this trip. It wasn't pedestrianized and prettied up for tourists. It was overrun with epically congested traffic, smoggy, grimy, and as it turned out, super dangerous.

Alyssa, who'd shared a taxi with us from the airport, said goodbye and set off to walk the two blocks to her nearby hotel alone. While this was happening, the hotel staff were orienting us, telling us about the features of the hotel, asking us when (not if) we were heading out to Machu Picchu. As they proudly pointed out the nearby Starbucks that could be accessed without having to walk outdoors on the street, it began to dawn on me that no tourist in their right mind would stay in this part of town, because the streets out there were very mean.

As Nora and I settled down to catch up on some much-needed sleep, I had a pang of guilt about Alyssa. Why had we let her walk to her hotel alone? I hoped she was okay.

Unfortunately, she was not.

The phone rang minutes later. It was Alyssa. She'd been mugged.

Oh no! What a disaster! Her purse stolen! How was she going to get home the next day without a passport?

But when she came into our room a few minutes later, I saw that her purse hadn't been stolen, she still had it.

"Yeah, a guy grabbed it and tried to yank it out of my hands," she said. "But I wasn't going to just let him!"

"Of course not," I said, marveling at the wonder that was Alyssa, strength and courage and tenacity oozing out of her every pore.

"I mean, if he had a knife, maybe I would have let go..." She considered for a moment. "Naah. Flesh wounds heal."

She described the protracted game of tug-of-war that she and the mugger had played with her purse, how she'd eventually won, evaded his grasp and run into the nearby Starbucks, hiding out there until the coast was clear.

"Alyssa, you're staying here with us tonight," Nora said. "And nobody goes anywhere in Lima alone."

I felt tempted to say, "How bout nobody goes anywhere in Lima, period? Can we just hide out here in the hotel room and be safe?" Why did we need to see Lima? Ancient pyramid, whatever. Did we need to take the risk of putting ourselves out there as targets? Did we really want to get kidnapped at this late stage of the game?

"Let's get some sleep," Nora said. "Then we can go get dinner."

"And check out the venue," Alyssa added.

"And pick up those tickets," I said.

There we tickets that we had to pick up. Not Morrissey tickets. These were our train tickets to Machu Picchu, which, of course, couldn't be printed at home or picked up at the train station. That would be too easy. Instead, we had to go to a Peru Rail ticket booth in a mall in a faraway neighborhood to pick them up.

Fine. We were going to have to go out. We couldn't hide out in the safety of the hotel room. Safety is a trap, I reminded myself. If I wanted to be safe, I could have stayed at home. I wasn't going to let my courage fail me now. I was going to face Lima, and everything was going to be okay, because I wouldn't have to do it on my own.

The venue was an outdoor amphitheater in a nearby park, a setup that looked very similar to what we'd just had in Montevideo, but without the massive deep gulf separating the audience from the stage. Still, the barrier was too far from the stage for handshakes. The park looked nice, gated, with security guards keeping watch, so we decided it would be safe enough to aim to get on line after the sun rose, around 5am.

Just as we were leaving, we had the nice surprise of running into fellow fan, José from Mexico. He'd just come to town for this one show. We all took an Uber to Miraflores, the neighborhood where we had to pick up our tickets, and the difference between it and the gritty downtown was the difference between night and day. This side of Lima was lovely! Upscale stores and bars and hotels lined the streets. Everything was shiny and new and well-kept. We got pizza at a great vegetarian restaurant, and then went to pick up the tickets at Larcomar mall. Part of the mall was underground, part open-air. It was really nice, and we would have stayed longer if it wasn't getting late. It was time to get back. To give our Uber driver a landmark to pick us up at, we walked over to the JW Marriott across the street.

There was a crowd of young local people, about twenty of them, standing and sitting quietly near the entrance of the hotel. One of them looked at my sweatshirt and approached me.

"Are you with Morrissey?" he asked.

"No," I said. "I'm just here for the show. Why?"

I looked at all the expectant faces and it clicked.

"Oh my God, are you all waiting for him?" I asked. "You think he's staying here and you're waiting for him?"

The man nodded and grinned and unrolled a Morrissey poster that he hoped he'd get signed. Alyssa was doubtful that Morrissey would stay at a Marriott, but these people looked like they really knew something.

In the Uber on the way back to the hotel, traffic was slow, congested. We passed a sign on the highway that made us all smile—a bright video of Morrissey up on a billboard, advertising tomorrow night's show.

I thought about all the people sitting outside that Marriott, waiting. They weren't the only ones we'd seen. When we'd landed at the airport in Lima, a guy had broken away from a group of local fans and asked me if Morrissey had been on my flight, if I knew what time he was getting in.

"I have no idea," I told him.

"Did you see the band?" he said pointing to Boz and Matt and Gustavo, disappearing into their taxi.

"Sure," I said, utterly blasé, taking it all for granted. I'd seen them, I'd hugged them, we'd hung out. Of course. Why not?

But sitting in the Uber as it slowly made its way back downtown, it struck me anew what a huge gift Nora and I had been given, how none of it could be taken for granted. For almost two months, we'd gotten to see Morrissey twice a week. It was our routine, the life we lived now: get on a plane, go somewhere new, see Morrissey.

But that wasn't how it was for most people. These fans in Lima had been waiting for so long—and I didn't mean just since this morning at the airport. They had been waiting for years for Morrissey to return and fulfill the promise of the canceled 2013 tour. And it was all so close to happening. I could feel it in the air, the expectant hush, the whole city waiting for this amazing day that was about to dawn.

We went to sleep, and all too soon, the alarm was ringing and it was time to be up, out on the street, in the smoggy air of Lima, starting our long day on line.

Starting as it did at 5am, it was the longest day of queueing we'd done on the whole tour, but never had a day on line gone by so fast. All day long, there were people to talk to. Old friends, new friends, people who'd heard that we'd done the whole tour, and were curious to hear what it had been like.

Since I was one of the lucky five people who'd gotten to see the tour in its entirety, the question I was repeatedly asked was:

"Which show was the best one?"

It was an impossible question to answer. The best in which way? What scale was I measuring on?

Was it about the quality of the music? Then the answer was Luna Park. If it was about the passion and fervor of the audience, then it had to be Rio. There were strong arguments supporting each of these shows as being the very best. Teatro Opera in Buenos Aires was the most fun, best heckles. Yacht y Golf Club had been super heartwarming delight from start to finish. In Teatro Renault in São Paulo, I'd been bathed in Intimacy and gotten three hand-shakes from Morrissey. How did that not make it the best?

But still—still!—I couldn't choose. Because right from the start in Quito, it had all been perfect. With a baseline of perfec-tion, each show had been a variation on that theme, a different facet of beautiful wholeness being showcased each time. Perfect band, perfect Morrissey, perfect audience, brought together, each time they achieved a magic that made each show the abso-lute best.

There were moments—handshakes, or certain songs—that I would take away from this tour and treasure in my memory for the rest of my life. But the absolute best thing about this tour had really been nothing short of the whole tour—the experience of living it in its completeness.

Being asked to pick was like being asked, What's your favorite word in Speedway? It just didn't make sense to tear this tour into chunks and weigh them on a scale. Each show, yes, absolutely, had been wildly beautiful in and of itself. But what made the whole experience so special was having seen it all, having these shows placed in the context of each of these incredible South American cities, seen alongside thousands and thousands of su-per devoted fans, getting to stand on line all day in these differ-ent cultures and talk and share and sing, walking into venues, becoming part of that single entity that was the audience, time after time, country after country, throughout the whole of South America.

They say travel broadens the mind. But for me, this trip had broadened my heart. It had become big enough to take in a whole tour, seven countries, and most of all, the thousands and thousands of fans that I'd shared this with, an experience that would connect us in our hearts forever.

And here in Lima, waiting in the line that was getting longer and longer by the hour, snaking along the outside fence of the Parque de la Exposicion, of course, I loved all this too. Gritty and dirty and smoggy as Lima was, surrounded here by my giant Mozfamily, I wished that we'd had more time. More time to see Lima, more time  to take in more than these tiny sips of all the places we'd been, more time to nurture the friendships that had begun with so many amazing fans. But this was it, the final moments of the tour just around the corner.

That last day on line, there were two highlights. The first was Chayane. He'd been such a fun person to be around all throughout the tour. He'd been so funny and smart, always willing to help us out with great little tidbits of knowledge about the cities we were visiting. In return, we'd always shared our vegan snacks with him. Often nothing more exciting than crackers or potato chips, but he'd always seemed to appreciate it.

Here in Lima, he appeared with a big bag of takeout and opened it up in front of me and Nora.

"This is to pay you back for all the times you fed me on this tour."

He took out dish after delicious dish from Lima's best vegan restaurant Sabor y Vida, a place that everyone who'd been to Lima for the aborted 2013 tour had raved about, but Nora and I had resigned ourselves to never visiting because it was only open for lunch and we just couldn't squeeze it in. But now Sabor y Vida had come to us. The dishes were vegan recreations of traditional Peruvian favorites. Beef and rice and vegetables and potatoes. Ceviche. Beef hearts on skewers. My God, heavenly stuff. So great.

And the second highlight happened when I was walking back from the hotel with Alyssa and Brazilian fan Juli late in the afternoon. As we approached the park, we heard music. Sound check! This was an outdoor venue, so it was crystal clear. But oh, wait. What was this? Could it be?

Yes! It wasn't just the band. Morrissey was singing! Oh this was too much fun! Walking, no, dancing down the street in Lima to the sound of Morrissey serenading the town with This Charming Man. I could feel it in my bones, he was happy.

We had joined Nora on line by now and I slipped in beside her and took her hand. Here we were, standing outside the venue of the twelfth and final show of the tour. And inside that venue, singing, was Morrissey.

"Do you know what this means?" I whispered into Nora's ear. "We made it. Me, you and Morrissey. We made it. To all twelve shows."

Back when we'd been planning this trip, it had seemed so unlikely that it would happen, that everything would work out. But it was happening, our little miracle had been granted.

We grinned at each other, and then started to crack up when we heard the next song that came from inside the venue. Could it be? Was that really the sound of pan pipes?

"I'd rather be a sparrow than a snail," Morrissey began.

What the hell? El Condor Pasa? I was brought back to Quito, where we'd encountered this song at every turn. It had been so ubiquitous, it had turned into a joke. And now Morrissey was singing it? This was too hilarious!

"He's not going to sing that tonight," Alyssa said.

"Oh yes he is," I said. "They're not just jamming. That's Gustavo playing the pan pipes. That's the sound of a rehearsal right there."

"No!' she said.

"Yes!" I said.

"Bet you everything I've got," Alyssa said. "Seven soles he doesn't sing it."

"What's that, like two dollars?" I said. "You're on!"

As we got closer to doors, security lined up right outside the entrance to the amphitheater. We stepped forward for our last bag search, handed over our last tickets, made the last mad dash into the venue to secure our spots on the barrier. We went for the Jesse and Gustavo side, just to spend a little bit more time with them while we could.

Looking across the half-circle of the curved barrier, I could see everyone: Trinity, Chayane, Alyssa, Doug, Juli, Vanessa, Alejandro and Jorge and all the South American crowd who'd followed a bunch of the tour. And over on my other side, Elina who was standing beside Grace, who'd popped in from Atlanta for one more show. We smiled and waved at each other. Charles Aznavour appeared on the screen and serenaded us with Emmenez-Moi one last time. I was going to miss this, miss all of it.

The waiting finally came to an end. The dramatic music played that heralded Morrissey's arrival on stage. Once again, for the last time, the crowd gelled, coalesced, became the single entity that was the audience for this show.

Morrissey and the band appeared and took their customary bow and the excitement around me hit fever pitch. The whole place was screaming and whistling. Glancing over my shoulder, the audience in the steeply pitched auditorium was a sea of hands reaching, reaching towards the stage.

Morrissey approached the microphone.

"My Lima! My Lima! My Lima!" he said, and for the last time launched into Suedehead.

"Why do you come here?" he asked us.

Every voice in the place was singing along. Every time Morrissey paused, even just for a second or two at the end of a verse, the space was filled with screams and cheers. The whole place felt like it was filled with Suedehead all the way up to the night sky above us. Morrissey prowled around the stage, whipping the microphone cord here and there to emphasize a line. The band played like champions, hitting every note with precision and power. Jesse came forward to the edge of the stage right in front of us to strut his stuff during his solos. Everyone looked so happy—the band, Morrissey. And all of us in the audience? Well, we were delirious.

"Gracias," Morrissey said after Suedehead. "You are welcome to everything I have."

After Suedehead came Alma Matters, Speedway and Ganglord.

Here were songs that we'd heard all throughout the tour. But tonight, there was something extraordinary about them. It was

as if the energy of the whole tour possessed the songs, made them more themselves than they had ever been.

This was very much the case as they launched into Ganglord. It was a wildly fantastic rendition, we were all howling the chorus to the heavens.

"And I'm turning to you to save me! Save me! Save me! Save me!"

This was it, the massive finale, nothing held back.

And then, there was a very special interlude. Gustavo took out his pan pipes, a picture of a tabby cat appeared on the screen, and Morrissey said, "I would now like to sing a song very, very badly."

El Condor Pasa, I now understand, is an extremely precious and meaningful song to the people of Peru, Ecuador and the whole Andean region. It is considered to be Peru's second

national anthem. When Paul Simon ripped it off and added his
goofy lyrics in English, he was really nicking some top-drawer
stuff.

So if it ever came around again, if I was ever at another Morrissey show in Lima, and Gustavo took out his pan pipes and
Morrissey started singing about the sparrow and the snail and
the hammer and the nail, I would totally behave. I would respect
the Andean culture which I adore, and I would listen attentively,
granting the song the gravitas that it truly deserves.

That's not what happened the first time around though. I
have to confess that I laughed and laughed. Gustavo was playing
pan pipes! Morrissey was singing a goofy Simon and Garfunkel
song! And what was Matt Walker doing on the drums! It was too
much! Before I expired from delighted mirth, they segued into
How Soon Is Now? This was the second national anthem of Morrisseyland, and all citizens present sang their hearts out.

Here we were, it was happening again: perfect band, perfect
Morrissey, perfect audience. It was the final encounter, our last
hurrah, the closing installment of a tour that had been perfection
from first to last.

And this show lacked nothing on the perfection front. Each
song was delivered to us so fully and completely. Each song swept
us all away. We swam in the beauty of First of the Gang. We were
happily drowned in Everyday Is Like Sunday.

"Share some grease tea with me," Morrissey sang and we all
sang along. "Every day is silent and grey."

How many times had I heard him sing those lines? How
many times had he sung them? It didn't matter. Infused with the
power of his heart, they were brought to us fresh and simple, yet
so full of meaning.

After that, so lovely, came The World Is Full of Crashing
Bores. I reached for Nora, and with her arms around me, my
heart full of gratitude, I sang the words that were no longer true:

"The world is full, so full of crashing bores, and I must be one, cos no one ever turns to me to say, take me in your arms, take me in your arms, and love me."

As we sang, Morrissey came up to the edge of the stage near us, and with one arm each around each other, we reached our free hands out to Morrissey, letting the gratitude and love pour out of us up onto the stage. It felt like Nora and I had one heart reaching out to his, thanking him for everything that he had given us—the inspiration, the courage, the knowledge that our hearts were not alone, no matter how dark the long night was. And all the people around us, our hearts were one with theirs too. All of us part of one big heart, reaching up to Morrissey, beating in time with the music.

How could a night like this come to be? I looked around me—really looked—at the audience I was a part of. It had never stopped, not from the moment Morrissey had stepped onto the stage. Everyone was standing on benches, leaning forward, arms reaching, singing, every fiber of them straining towards Morrissey. Their hearts were shining in their eyes, tingling in their outstretched fingertips.

And Morrissey? The fullness of his beautiful heart was poured into every word he sang. This too, had never stopped since the moment he'd stepped on stage tonight. But it wasn't just tonight. His heart had been poured into every syllable of every song of this tour. Every single time, all the way from Quito, he had sung to us holding his heart in his hands, offering it to us, the audience.

The show was winding towards its inevitable conclusion. It should have been a bittersweet thing to hear Morrissey sing I Will See You in Far Off Places. Here was the last of the far off places we were seeing him. It was all ending so soon.

"But there is no end," he sang, "And I will see you…"

And it was true. The connection of the heart was something that triumphed over time. And still and still, as the songs counted down, we felt it, time, nipping at our heels. Any second now, Morrissey would leave and be gone forever. His heart, his presence, was something that was here just for now. Here on this magic night. Here for this whole tour. A gift he was offering to us, his audience.

And oh, how South America had seen the gift he was giving, taken it in, and responded. Standing here, again for the last time, I watched and felt the exquisitely tender exchange. Artist and audience, offering their hearts to each other, touching and being touched, held together in the arms of music that meant everything, said all the words the heart needed to say.

And this was it. The final embrace between Morrissey and his South American audience, every moment filled to the brim with sweetness and passion, only a few seconds left in which all could be expressed.

"Let me kiss you," Morrissey sang, his last song before he left the stage. "Let me kiss you."

And then he was gone.

"We have had a fantastic time in South America," he said when he came back for the encore. "It's been an incredible tour for us, we're very grateful. We thank our beloved crew and we thank beloved Peru."

And with The Queen Is Dead, we raced through the final minutes of the tour, coming to that one last flourish, crash, definitive chord that said, Now, at last, it is over!

When all is said and done, what remains?

We went to Machu Picchu the next day. We took a plane, a car, a train, and finally a bus up the final hair-raising, switchbacked road to the citadel. We handed over tickets at the turnstile, tickets I had bought two months before, hardly daring to believe that it could all work out, that everything would go according to plan and we would make it to this place on this date.

But here we were, just in time, the show was about to start.

It was wet, misty. We were up so high, clouds were moving below in the valley between us and the mountains before us. Up so high, all reason was gone, it was just the mountains, the beauty of them, standing at the barrier, looking.

And then, a rainbow started to grow. It reached across, building itself, making a bridge between one mountain and the other. Magic. The clouds moved and it dispersed again. Nora and I

moved on too. We followed the path to another barrier, again the vista of the mountains before us, the deep gulf between us and them.

The rainbow started to re-form. It reached between the two mountains. It stretched beyond. We were up so high, we were looking at it from above. It began to paint itself onto the valley floor, the trees lit up beneath it.

"It's the end of the rainbow," I said. "There's a pot of gold down there!"

"Inca gold," Nora said.

Stronger and stronger, the rainbow made headway on both sides. It was almost alarming, it seemed determined to reach out to us, to cross the gulf, to encircle us. But of course it couldn't make it all the way.

"You know what I'm doing now?" Nora said. "I'm doing the equivalent of giving it a handshake."

"Yes," I said. "Good idea. Me too."

We stood at the barrier and our hearts reached out across the gulf. Love, awe, wonder, it was all there. But most of all, there was gratitude. Gratitude for everything we'd seen, gratitude for the connections our hearts had made, gratitude for the magically beautiful thing that had been Morrissey's tour of South America.

16739043R00140

Printed in Great Britain
by Amazon